MTEL®

Reading Specialist Practice Questions

I0877310

Mometrix
TEST PREPARATION

DEAR FUTURE EXAM SUCCESS STORY

First of all, **THANK YOU** for purchasing Mometrix study materials!

Second, congratulations! You are one of the few determined test-takers who are committed to doing whatever it takes to excel on your exam. **You have come to the right place.** We developed these practice tests with one goal in mind: to deliver you the best possible approximation of the questions you will see on test day.

Standardized testing is one of the biggest obstacles on your road to success, which only increases the importance of doing well in the high-pressure, high-stakes environment of test day. Your results on this test could have a significant impact on your future, and these practice tests will give you the repetitions you need to build your familiarity and confidence with the test content and format to help you achieve your full potential on test day.

Your success is our success

We would love to hear from you! If you would like to share the story of your exam success or if you have any questions or comments in regard to our products, please contact us at **800-673-8175** or **support@mometrix.com**.

Thanks again for your business and we wish you continued success!

Sincerely,
The Mometrix Test Preparation Team

Printed in the United States of America

Table of Contents

Practice Test #1

Multiple Choice Questions

1. A first-grade teacher schedules 10 minutes each day for sight word practice. This daily practice will most likely improve students' reading proficiency by building which skill?

a. Decoding
b. Automaticity
c. Phonemic awareness
d. Phonological awareness

2. A teacher observes a first-grade student as she writes the word *stop* in her journal. The student says each sound out loud before writing the corresponding letter on her paper. Which process is the student exhibiting?

a. Blending
b. Decoding
c. Segmenting
d. Encoding

3. While reading a book about animals, a student struggles to decode the word *giraffe*. He then points to the picture and says, "Those are giraffes. I saw them at the zoo." Which cueing system is the student using to figure out the unknown word?

a. Semantic
b. Syntactic
c. Graphophonic
d. Pragmatic

4. Which statement best describes the relationship between phonological awareness and phonemic awareness?

a. Phonological awareness and phonemic awareness are interchangeable terms.
b. Phonological awareness is one specific component of phonemic awareness.
c. Phonemic awareness is one specific component of phonological awareness.
d. Phonological awareness typically develops after phonemic awareness.

5. A preschool teacher has identified a small group of students who are lacking any phonological awareness skills. Which skill would be most appropriate for the teacher to initially focus on during small-group instruction?

a. Syllabification
b. Segmenting onsets and rimes
c. Blending
d. Rhyming

6. Liz, a third grader, is completing a reading assessment with her teacher. During the fluency component of the assessment, she reads a short passage aloud. Her teacher notes that Liz's reading rate is in the average range for her grade level, and she correctly decodes 95% of the words in the passage. However, Liz reads in a monotone voice and often forgets to pause before beginning new sentences. Which component of fluency should Liz's teacher target during small-group instruction?

a. Accuracy
b. Automaticity
c. Word recognition
d. Prosody

7. Which statement best describes phonemic awareness?

a. Phonemic awareness is the ability to identify and manipulate sounds at the sentence level.
b. Phonemic awareness is the ability to identify and manipulate sounds at the word level.
c. Phonemic awareness is the ability to identify and manipulate sounds at the syllable level.
d. Phonemic awareness is the ability to identify and manipulate sounds at the phoneme level.

8. During a small-group activity, a teacher asks her students to repeat a CVC word slowly, stretching out the sounds. As students repeat the word, they slide one penny forward for each sound they hear. Which phonemic awareness skill are students practicing?

a. Blending
b. Segmenting
c. Phoneme identification
d. Phoneme isolation

9. Which choice represents a likely progression of phonological awareness skills?

a. Onset and rime manipulation, rhyming, phoneme deletion, syllabification
b. Phoneme deletion, syllabification, onset and rime manipulation, rhyming
c. Rhyming, syllabification, onset and rime manipulation, phoneme deletion
d. Syllabification, phoneme deletion, rhyming, onset and rime manipulation

10. A preschool teacher is reading aloud to his students using a big book. He wants to help his students understand that the print carries the meaning of the story. What can the teacher do to foster this understanding?

a. Show students where to start reading on each page
b. Point to the words while reading
c. Model the return sweep at the end of each line of text
d. Ask students what they see in the pictures

11. A teacher asks her students to say the word *map*. She then says, "Change the /m/ sound to a /t/ sound. What word do you have now?" Which phonemic awareness skill are students practicing?

a. Alliteration
b. Segmenting
c. Blending onset and rime
d. Phoneme substitution

12. Which of the following options best describes the use of environmental print in a prekindergarten classroom?

a. Including real food packages and menus in the dramatic play area
b. Setting aside 10 minutes each day for students to read books independently
c. Displaying sight words on a word wall
d. Creating anchor charts of vocabulary words from content areas

13. Alex is a first-grade student. His teacher notices that he commonly substitutes words that make sense in the sentences but don't match the print. For example, he recently said, "The car drove down a street," while the text actually said, "The car drove down the street." Which cueing system is Alex using?

a. Graphophonic
b. Semantic
c. Syntactic
d. Pragmatic

14. Mrs. Lopez teaches second grade. After completing a science experiment, she gathers her students on the carpet to write a summary of what they learned. Mrs. Lopez asks students to help her record the responses on chart paper, sharing the marker. She provides guidance and sentence starters as needed. After everyone has recorded their responses, the class reads them aloud together. Which type of writing experience is Mrs. Lopez demonstrating?

a. Interactive writing
b. Shared writing
c. Independent writing
d. Guided writing

15. Mr. Johnson is a sixth-grade language arts teacher. He wants to help his students assess their own growth in writing skills over the course of the year. Which type of assessment method would most likely help Mr. Johnson achieve his goal?

a. Norm-referenced writing tests
b. Criterion-referenced writing tests
c. Performance-based tasks
d. Writing portfolios

16. Ms. Peterson is reading a big book to her kindergarten students. She shows them where the title and author's name are located on the cover. She then tracks the text with her finger as she reads. What is Ms. Peterson modeling for her students?

a. Concepts of print
b. Phonological awareness
c. Phonemic awareness
d. Close reading

17. Michael is a sixth-grade student who struggles to summarize fictional texts he has read. His summaries are often lengthy and include many unimportant details. Which type of graphic organizer could best help Michael develop concise summaries?

a. KWL charts
b. Semantic maps
c. Venn diagrams
d. Story maps

18. Which classroom instructional strategy would most likely assist ELLs with developing phonemic awareness skills?

a. Practicing phonemic awareness skills on familiar vocabulary words in English
b. Practicing phonemic awareness skills using only words in their native languages
c. Introducing phonemes that are not part of their native languages first
d. Teaching the English alphabet and alphabetic principle before teaching phonemic awareness skills

19. What is one benefit of implicit phonics instruction?

a. It leads to stronger decoding skills.
b. Its progression from part to whole increases proficiency more quickly.
c. Research suggests it is the most effective approach to phonics instruction.
d. Phonics skills are taught in a meaningful context.

20. Mr. Clark is conducting a daily phonics lesson. Today, the class is focusing on the *st* consonant blend. Students first repeatedly produce the sound the blend makes. They then search for *st* words within the classroom. Which approach to phonics instruction is Mr. Clark demonstrating?

a. Implicit
b. Explicit
c. Whole language
d. Analytical

21. Ms. Watson has included a variety of pointers in the classroom reading center. She instructs students to use these pointers or their fingers to point to the words when reading independently. Which of the following concepts of print is Ms. Watson addressing?

a. Spacing
b. Book orientation
c. Directionality
d. Letter concepts

22. Which of the following activities best demonstrates a multisensory approach to teaching letter formation?

a. Locating words containing a certain letter in a book
b. Tracing prewritten letters on paper with a pencil
c. Identifying letters on flashcards
d. Writing letters in shaving cream

23. Kindergarten students learn one new letter and its corresponding sound each week. They participate in songs and chants that include repetitive use of the letter name and sound. Which concept are students practicing?

a. Alphabetic principle
b. Concepts of print
c. Phonological awareness
d. Automaticity

24. Which of the following words contains an r-controlled vowel?

a. Rock
b. Short
c. Rain
d. Trace

25. Which of the following words contains a consonant digraph?

a. Swim
b. Blue
c. From
d. Cheek

26. Which activity would be most appropriate to teach decoding of CVCe words?

a. Covering parts of the word
b. Chunking
c. Building word families
d. Blending

27. Which strategy can be used to build readers' confidence and increase both comprehension and fluency when introducing an unknown text?

a. Introducing new vocabulary before reading
b. Reading the first few pages aloud before asking students to finish it independently
c. Listing what students want to learn about the topic
d. Asking students to predict what the text will be about based on the title and cover

28. A second-grade reading teacher notices that her students are decoding words accurately but struggle with appropriate phrasing and expression. Which activity would most likely help her students improve in this area?

a. Introducing new texts of varied genres for students to read aloud independently
b. Listening to audio versions of texts
c. Leading students in repeated choral readings of familiar texts
d. Participating in partner-reading experiences

29. Which of the following linguistic domains relates primarily to the meanings of words?

a. Graphophonic
b. Semantic
c. Syntactic
d. Pragmatic

30. Children first begin their vocabulary development using which skill?

a. Reading
b. Writing
c. Listening
d. Speaking

31. How does environmental print contribute to reading development?

a. It helps children apply the alphabetic principle.
b. It often contains words that are easily decodable.
c. It models one-to-one correspondence.
d. It helps children understand that print contains meaning.

32. Mr. Suarez teaches a preschool class containing students in the preliterate stage of writing. He wants to help his students understand the relationship between spoken and written words using a familiar topic, so he has planned an activity relating to the class's recent field trip to the apple orchard. Mr. Suarez will help the group record memories of their field trip in writing while they contribute ideas, and Mr. Suarez will read the writing back to students repeatedly throughout the week. Which activity would be most appropriate?

a. Shared writing
b. Independent writing
c. Interactive writing
d. Partner writing

33. Before asking students to read a new fiction book independently, the teacher conducts a picture walk with the class. What is the teacher's primary goal for conducting the picture walk?

a. Encouraging the use of syntactic cues
b. Setting a purpose for reading
c. Activating students' prior knowledge
d. Developing students' metacognitive skills

34. A first-grade teacher wants to help students compare and contrast short vowel sounds. Which activity would best assist students with this skill?

a. Segmenting words with short vowel sounds using Elkonin boxes
b. Tracing words with short vowel sounds using stencils
c. Sorting words containing short vowel sounds
d. Including words with short vowel sounds on the weekly spelling list

35. Which of the following examples best describes explicit and systematic phonics instruction?

a. A teacher observes a student as he reads a book independently. When the student struggles to decode a word with a certain spelling pattern, the teacher intervenes and provides a mini-lesson on the skill.
b. A teacher assesses her students' phonics skills regularly and uses the assessment data to plan flexible, targeted, small-group instruction on specific sounds and blends.
c. A teacher conducts frequent surveys to learn more about her students' interests. She uses the results to select books on these topics. She then identifies a few phonics skills that can be taught using the text in each book.
d. A teacher reads a big book aloud to her students. She stops on a page and asks students if they notice any patterns in the words. Students identify words that start with the same letter, end with the same suffixes, and more. The teacher briefly explains each of their observations.

36. A group of students is playing a card game at a classroom reading center. They take turns flipping over two cards and trying to create matches. Each match consists of a letter and a picture of a word that begins with that letter. For example, a student matches a card containing a letter *p* and a card displaying a picture of a pig. What concept are students practicing?

a. Encoding
b. One-to-one correspondence
c. Phoneme isolation
d. Alphabetic principle

37. A teacher asks her students to say /ake/. She then tells students to add different consonant sounds to the beginning of /ake/ to see which real and nonsense words they can form. Which component of phonological awareness are students practicing in this activity?

a. Syllabification
b. Onsets and rimes
c. Phoneme isolation
d. Segmentation

38. What is the first step that families and caregivers can take to encourage language development in children after birth?

a. Forming rhyming words
b. Creating a print-rich environment
c. Talking and singing to the child frequently
d. Pointing out environmental print

39. A third-grade student has difficulties with decoding and struggles to read grade-level texts independently. Which statement is likely to be true based on this information?

a. The student will benefit from additional implicit phonics instruction.
b. The student will also struggle with phonological awareness.
c. The student will also struggle with fluency and comprehension.
d. The student likely has a language processing disorder and requires further evaluation.

Refer to the following for question 40:

A fourth-grade student struggles to decode several words in her science textbook, including *organism*, *conclusion*, and *prediction*.

40. Which strategy would best help the student decode these and other similar words?

a. Using context clues to select words that make sense in the sentences
b. Slowly stretching out the letter sounds
c. Blending the phonemes
d. Looking for known word parts, such as prefixes and suffixes

41. What is a morpheme?

a. The smallest unit of language with meaning
b. The smallest unit of speech
c. A letter or group of letters representing a single sound
d. A unit of spoken language in a word, which contains a single vowel sound

42. Which sentence contains a homophone pair?

a. When I multitask, I perform multiple jobs at once.
b. When you go to the picnic, you should park your car on the east side of the park.
c. Our team won the game by scoring a touchdown with one minute left on the clock.
d. There were many bees flying among the trees.

43. Which of the following words contains a prefix?

a. Cooking
b. Mist
c. Trap
d. Mislead

44. A sixth-grade science teacher wants to help his students recognize connections between words containing the same Latin root. Which activity would most likely achieve this goal?

a. Defining words containing the root using a dictionary
b. Creating a semantic map
c. Searching for words containing the root in the science textbook
d. Comparing and contrasting words containing the root using a Venn diagram

45. A teacher gives students a list of words, including *care*, *home*, and *use*, and asks them to record the definitions. Next, she asks them to add *less* to the ends of the words and record the new definitions. Students are then instructed to write down their observations in their writing journals. What is the primary purpose of this activity?

a. Helping students recognize the meaning of a common suffix
b. Teaching students the *-less* spelling pattern
c. Practicing word analysis skills that will assist with decoding
d. Identifying commonly used prefixes

46. What are homographs?

a. Words that are spelled differently but pronounced the same way
b. Words that are spelled the same way but have different meanings
c. Words that have the same Latin root
d. Words that are members of the same word family

47. Maria, a third-grade student, is reading a new chapter book for the first time. Her teacher observes as Maria struggles to decode the word *scapegoat* in the following sentence: "John frowned when he realized he was being made the scapegoat." Which of the following strategies would most likely assist Maria with decoding this word?

a. Using syntactic cues
b. Blending the sounds
c. Using context clues from the sentence
d. Chunking

48. A student is reading a fictional book and reaches the following sentence: "Unlike Mark, whose college plans were tentative, Ana already had firm plans to attend the state university." Which type of context clue is present in this sentence to help the student determine the meaning of *tentative*?

a. Synonym clue
b. Definition clue
c. Antonym clue
d. Inference clue

49. Cognates and realia are most useful for teaching which component of reading instruction to ELLs?

a. Vocabulary
b. Prosody
c. Phonological awareness
d. Phonemic awareness

50. "It's raining cats and dogs" is an example of which type of expression?

a. Idiom
b. Proverb
c. Simile
d. Metaphor

51. Prior to launching a sixth-grade genre study on historical fiction, Mrs. Perez plans to create a list of vocabulary words to explicitly teach to her students. She wants to select tier-two words that will best contribute to students' overall language development and allow them to transfer their knowledge to other reading experiences. Which words fit these criteria?

a. Challenging but common vocabulary words that carry a lot of meaning
b. High-frequency, concrete nouns
c. Domain-specific words found in students' social studies textbooks
d. Student-selected words related to their interests within the genre

52. A teacher wants to help her students develop metacognitive skills. Which guiding question can she prompt students to ask themselves while reading?

a. Who are the major and minor characters?
b. Were my predictions correct?
c. What happened first?
d. What is the theme of the story?

53. A teacher wants to help his students compare and contrast two main characters within a fictional story. Which graphic organizer should he use to best help students achieve this objective?

a. Venn diagram
b. Story map
c. Five W's chart
d. T-chart

54. Students in a sixth-grade classroom are preparing to deliver a persuasive speech to school administrators requesting additional playground equipment. As part of their preparations, students are learning to adjust the formality of their spoken language to match specific situations. In small groups, they are role playing how they would make requests to friends, teachers, and administrators. They are comparing and contrasting the appropriate language to use in each situation. Which oral language component are students practicing?

a. Morphology
b. Semantics
c. Syntax
d. Pragmatics

55. A teacher gives students an unfamiliar text. Without doing a picture walk or pre-teaching any vocabulary words, she asks them to read it once independently. During this first reading, students are told to identify the overall meaning of the text, as well as note their initial impressions. Students discuss these responses with their peers. The teacher then asks the students to read a specific portion of the text a second time, analyzing the author's use of figurative language. Students then discuss their thoughts again. The teacher then asks the students to reread the text a third time, comparing and contrasting the main character with the main character in another text they have read. Students once again share their responses with peers. Which type of reading activity does this example demonstrate?

a. Guided reading
b. SQ3R
c. Close reading
d. Scanning

56. A teacher gives students a story map to complete while reading a realistic fiction text. They are asked to record the characters, setting, problem, events, and solution. Which level of comprehension does this activity address?

a. Affective
b. Literal
c. Inferential
d. Evaluative

57. Students in a sixth-grade classroom are reading a persuasive essay about the importance of recycling. Which question can the teacher ask to help students develop evaluative comprehension skills?

a. Do you agree with the author that recycling is an easy way for everyone to help the environment?
b. Which material takes longer to decompose: plastic or glass?
c. What types of materials can be recycled?
d. Who should you contact in your city if you want to help organize a recycling program?

58. A teacher wants to help his students identify the types of nonfiction texts they are reading based on their text structures. Which keywords would students likely find in compare-and-contrast texts?

a. For example and for instance
b. Similarly and on the other hand
c. Because and as a result
d. First, next, and finally

59. Students in Ms. Dean's class discuss their existing knowledge and thoughts about sustainable farming practices before conducting any research on the topic. Next, they research the topic, locating four reputable print sources and conducting one interview with an expert in the field. They take notes, recording key information from each source. They use their notes from all of the sources to write a research report on the topic. They also complete a written reflection outlining how their initial thoughts have changed as a result of the new information gathered from the sources. Which comprehension strategy are students demonstrating?

a. Evaluating
b. Inferring
c. Drawing conclusions
d. Synthesizing

60. Students in a fourth-grade classroom read a novel about Alicia, a character who moves from a farm to a big city and struggles with the resulting changes in her lifestyle. After reading and discussing the text together, the teacher asks students to make a text-to-self connection. Which student response demonstrates a text-to-self connection?

a. Alicia reminds me a lot of Jacob in the book we read last semester. His family moved across the globe, and he had to adapt to the cultural differences in his new home.
b. I saw a story on the news about a girl who moved to a big city, and she helped set up a community garden in her new neighborhood.
c. Last year, I had to attend a new school because my family bought a new house in the city. It was hard at first to make new friends because everyone else already knew each other.
d. This was one of my favorite books we read this year because Alicia learned to make the best out of a difficult situation.

61. Aidan, a fifth-grade student, writes a letter to the cafeteria manager at his school asking her to implement a schoolwide composting program. He outlines reasons why the composting program would benefit the environment and save the school money on waste disposal costs. He ends his letter by politely asking her to consider the proposal. What is Aidan's primary purpose for writing?

a. To inform
b. To persuade
c. To entertain
d. To describe

62. Based on assessment data, a teacher identifies a small group of students who would benefit from targeted instruction on using textual evidence to support their answers. Which strategy would be most helpful for the teacher to model to assist students with this type of test question?

a. Underlining passages in the text where answers are located
b. Reading the passage once to identify the main idea, and then rereading to look for details
c. Reading each answer choice carefully before selecting an answer, crossing out answers as they are eliminated
d. Completing a story map while reading the story

63. Kelsey is writing a descriptive essay about the rainforest for her science class. Which graphic organizer can she use during the prewriting process to best help her plan her essay?

a. Sequencing chart
b. Sensory chart
c. T-chart
d. Persuasion map

64. A teacher wants to incorporate a lesson on point of view into his class's fairy tale genre study. Which activity would best accomplish this goal?

a. Reading a modern-day fairy tale and asking students to record what they liked and didn't like about the story in their journals
b. Contrasting two versions of the same fairy tale narrated by two different characters
c. Having students write a different ending to an existing fairy tale
d. Comparing and contrasting the events in a fractured fairy tale and its traditional version

65. Which of the following represents a main difference between the conventions of spoken and written language?

a. Syntax is more relaxed in spoken language, with more flexibility in word order.
b. Body language plays a bigger role in sharing meaning in written language than in spoken language.
c. Written language tends to be less formal and more conversational in nature than spoken language.
d. Written language includes a greater mixture of fragments and complete sentences than spoken language.

66. A teacher asks students to close their eyes while she reads a descriptive, fictional text aloud. When she is done reading, students draw pictures of the story's setting and share their pictures with the class. Which reading strategy are students practicing?

a. Predicting
b. Inferring
c. Summarizing
d. Visualizing

67. A struggling reader has difficulty comprehending vocabulary words when they are encountered in unfamiliar texts. She frequently uses a dictionary to look up the unknown words. While this helps her figure out the meanings of the words, it interrupts her fluency and affects comprehension. Her teacher, Mr. Palmer, would like to teach her other strategies she can use instead that will minimize the disruptions to her fluency and increase her comprehension. Which strategy would likely be most effective?

a. Quickly asking a classmate for the meanings of the words
b. Creating a list of the unknown words and looking them up later
c. Trying to determine the meanings of the words from context clues
d. Skipping over the words she does not know as long as the sentences make sense

68. A fourth-grade teacher gives students a character chart to fill out while reading a fictional text. Students are instructed to record traits of the main character as they read. One student, Daniel, turns in a map that lists the following traits: short, has blond hair, has freckles, is a girl. Which strategy would be an appropriate next step for the teacher to focus on?

a. Analyzing character development from the beginning of the story to the end
b. Identifying the character as a protagonist or antagonist
c. Differentiating between internal and external character traits
d. Comparing and contrasting the character with a character from another book by the same author

69. Meg is preparing an expository research report to share information about the costs involved in pet ownership. She shares information she printed from a website during her research that she plans to incorporate into her report. The website states, "Even though having a dog requires a significant amount of time and attention, I believe it is definitely worth it. Everyone should have a pet dog because they are the most loyal friends you will ever find." Which of the following would be the most appropriate topic for a mini-lesson based on Meg's current plans?

a. Synthesizing information from multiple sources
b. Choosing between a descriptive and compare/contrast text structure
c. Using headings and other expository text features
d. Differentiating between facts and opinions

70. Students in the transitional stage of reading development would benefit most from instruction in which area?

a. Sight word practice
b. Identifying the theme of abstract texts
c. Analyzing morphology to determine word meanings
d. Letter/sound correspondence

71. A teacher wants to select books for her emergent readers to add to the classroom library. Which set of text features are most appropriate for emergent readers?

a. Predictable text placement, repetition, and picture support
b. Complex and varied sentence types, multiple sentences per page, little picture support
c. Sidebars and charts, several lines of text per page, descriptive words and phrases
d. Complex text structures, figurative language, technical vocabulary words

72. Students in Mr. Henderson's science class are conducting research for their science fair projects. Today, they are typing keywords into a search engine to identify sources that may be relevant for their background information. Which reading strategy should Mr. Henderson teach and practice with his students prior to this activity?

a. Skimming
b. Scanning
c. Close reading
d. Extensive reading

73. Tyler, a first-grade student, read a new book to his teacher while she took a running record. The teacher determined that Tyler read the text with 93% accuracy. The teacher noted that while Tyler struggled to decode a few challenging words in the text, he used strategies to accurately decode the remaining words. Based on this information, the book would be at which reading level for Tyler?

a. Frustration level
b. Instructional level
c. Independent level
d. Lexile level

74. Which of the following options best represents a research-based approach to reading instruction?

a. Students within a class rotate through a series of reading centers each day. One center is at the teacher's table. All students in the class read the same text during their time with the teacher but receive individualized assistance and instruction due to the small-group setting.
b. Students within a class read one story together from their textbook each week. They read the story multiple times and listen to a digital version. Students complete workbook activities to accompany the story. They also choose from other center activities.
c. Students are placed into reading groups at the beginning of each quarter based on assessment data. Groups rotate through a series of reading centers each day. Each group spends one rotation with the teacher reading a book chosen in consideration with the quarterly assessment data.
d. Students rotate through a series of reading centers each day. One center involves guided reading with the teacher using books in students' instructional reading levels. The groups are flexible and change frequently based on assessment data.

75. A teacher takes a running record while Charlie, a second grader, reads a new text. Part of the running record is shown below.

> home
> The witch's house was deep in the woods, hidden behind some
> grumpy
> trees. A grouchy cat guarded the entrance to the house, hissing
> omission
> loudly when any strangers approached. Nobody had dared to go
>
> near it in years.

Which strategy would be most appropriate for the teacher to focus on during the next guided reading session?

a. Using semantic cues
b. Using syntactic cues
c. Monitoring omissions
d. Making self-corrections

76. A teacher has concerns that a standardized test she is required to give does not accurately measure what it is designed to measure. The test claims to measure students' abilities to make inferences, yet there are no questions that directly address this skill. The teacher has concerns with which aspect of the standardized test?

a. Validity
b. Reliability
c. Bias
d. Objectivity

77. Which learning theory is based on the idea that students are actively involved in constructing their own meaning, and that teachers should guide students through scaffolding rather than using instructor-led teaching techniques?

a. Behaviorism
b. Cognitivism
c. Constructivism
d. Social learning theory

78. Which example best demonstrates a student learning in his zone of proximal development?

a. Being taught to apply a new decoding strategy while reading a book that contains some words that are new to the student
b. Casually practicing reading using a reading passage that the student is very familiar with
c. Listening to an audio version of a story in place of reading the written text because it is too difficult to read independently
d. Pairing up a stronger student with a struggling reader to model use of a comprehension strategy

79. Which example best demonstrates a student making an accommodation to existing schema, as suggested by Piaget?

a. A child knows that periods are used at the ends of sentences. When given a question to punctuate for the first time, she uses a period.
b. After using the writing process to write a narrative text, a child applies the process to write an expository text.
c. A child does not like bees until learning about the role they play in pollination. She then believes that bees are helpful.
d. A toddler learns about lions from a picture book and practices saying, "Roar!" She hears a tiger making a similar sound at the zoo and calls it a lion.

80. Which instructional strategy is most closely related to and is a key component of schema theory?

a. Summarizing
b. Activating prior knowledge
c. Identifying main idea
d. Recognizing story elements

81. The alphabetic principle would be best introduced at which of Piaget's cognitive stages of development?

a. Sensorimotor stage
b. Preoperational stage
c. Concrete operational stage
d. Formal operational stage

82. Which of the following options represents a key tenet of cognitivism?

a. Allowing social learning opportunities to foster cognitive development
b. Reinforcing desired behaviors so they continue
c. Chunking information to avoid cognitive overload
d. Encouraging students to be actively involved in constructing their own meaning

83. Which of the following examples best demonstrates teacher scaffolding?

a. A teacher gives students a mixture of building materials and challenges them to construct the tallest tower possible in 15 minutes.
b. A teacher reads a book related to the current science unit aloud because it is too difficult for students to read independently.
c. A teacher gives students time to self-select books related to their interests from the classroom library.
d. A teacher uses picture cards to pre-teach vocabulary before students read a new book independently.

84. Which classroom activity best demonstrates constructivism?

a. Students complete a close reading of a persuasive text using questions outlined by the teacher. They first read and discuss the main idea of the text. Next, they read and discuss the reasons the author provides to support her opinion. Finally, they reread the text and evaluate the author's effectiveness in persuading others to agree with her.
b. Students collaboratively decide to research costs and benefits of additional flexible seating options to the classroom, while the teacher assists with research strategies. Students then write a persuasive letter to the school board asking for funding for the seating.
c. Students complete a set of reading stations in a predetermined order. In one station, they complete phonics practice activities on the computer. In another, they match word cards to create compound words. In a third station, they sort words according to vowel sounds and check their work using an answer key.
d. Students in different grade levels are paired up. The older students read to the younger students and help them draw pictures of their favorite parts of the stories.

85. Which statement is a key tenet of Marie Clay's literacy processing theory?

a. Children have differing prior knowledge and previous experiences and take different paths to literacy development.
b. Literacy development is enhanced when children learn to write after developing basic reading skills.
c. Emergent readers learn best using large-group instruction, where they have models of proficient readers to emulate.
d. Children learn to read best with a whole-language approach to instruction, with little emphasis on assessment.

86. Sixth-grade students are taking a standardized, criterion-referenced reading test. Part of the test involves answering comprehension questions based on reading passages. Some of the passages contain cultural references that some groups of students do not understand, causing them to miss multiple questions. This is an example of a testing concern in which area?

a. Validity
b. Reliability
c. Bias
d. Consistency

87. What is one benefit of using a rubric over other types of assessment techniques?

a. Rubrics break down overall scores by criteria, allowing students to see their strengths and weaknesses.
b. Rubrics allow students to track their progress over time.
c. Rubrics help students see how they did in comparison with their peers.
d. Rubrics help identify the types of reading miscues students are making so teachers can provide targeted instruction.

88. What is a primary purpose for giving an Informal Reading Inventory to a student?

a. To track the texts and genres a student has read over the course of the school year
b. To help students identify books of personal interest
c. To determine which reading behaviors students have developed prior to entering formal schooling
d. To match students with appropriate instructional texts

89. Which statement best describes the relationship between reading and writing?

a. Reading is a prerequisite skill that should be taught before writing.
b. Writing is a prerequisite skill that should be taught before reading.
c. Reading and writing are interrelated and should be taught together.
d. The order of instruction does not matter, but one should be taught first to avoid cognitive overload.

Refer to the following for question 90:

For a poetry unit, a class is reading a 14-line poem in iambic pentameter. There are three stanzas of four lines each, and a two-line couplet at the end. Words at the end of each line rhyme with another word in the same stanza. After the first week of this unit, the teacher wants to determine if the instructional methods she is using are successful. If students are meeting the objectives introduced so far, she will continue with the strategies she is currently using. If students are struggling to meet the objectives, she will reteach them using a different approach. For the assessment, she plans to ask students to identify the literary devices she has introduced in sample poems.

90. Which type of assessment is the teacher planning to use?

a. Formative assessment
b. Summative assessment
c. Norm-referenced test
d. Screening assessment

91. Which of the following reading prompts requires the highest level of thinking, according to Bloom's taxonomy?

a. Compare and contrast the protagonist and antagonist in the story.
b. Evaluate the author's use of figurative language in conveying the theme of the story.
c. Identify the setting of the story.
d. Infer what the author means in the final paragraph of the story.

92. After students have studied metaphors for several days, a teacher wants to assess their abilities to apply their knowledge of what a metaphor is. Which assignment would be most appropriate for this purpose?

a. Underlining the metaphors in a sample text
b. Explaining what a metaphor is to a classmate
c. Writing a paragraph that includes at least two metaphors
d. Critiquing the author's use of metaphors in a poem

93. Which of the following aspects of reading comprehension belongs in the semantic language domain?

a. Grammar
b. Word order
c. Word meaning
d. Sentence structure

94. In addition to word frequency, sentence complexity, and vocabulary, which of the following factors is frequently used to level books?

a. Author's purpose
b. Interest level
c. Text features
d. Author's craft

95. A teacher wants to determine a student's accuracy and reading rate in order to determine if a text is in the student's frustration, instructional, or independent reading level. Which of the following assessments should she use?

a. Authentic assessment task
b. Rubric
c. Guided reading observation
d. Running record

96. What is one limitation of informal reading assessments?

a. They must be administered in a standardized fashion, increasing student anxiety.
b. The results may be subjective.
c. They require more time to plan and implement than formal assessments.
d. They are often costly to administer and score.

97. Which of the following options is an example of a formal reading assessment?

a. Student interviews
b. Guided reading observations
c. State reading test
d. Anecdotal records

98. Which of the following examples describes a summative assessment?

a. A lab report completed as a homework assignment
b. A weekly vocabulary quiz on science content words
c. A teacher's observations of a student as he completes a science experiment
d. A science test given at the end of a unit on adaptations

99. Timothy, a first-grade student, writes a few sentences in his reading journal.

February 8, I played in the rane on Tuzday. I wore a cote to stay dry. I saw a grene frog by the car.

Based on this writing sample, which skill should Timothy's teacher focus on first during small-group instruction?

a. Spelling days of the week
b. Consonant blends
c. Long vowel spelling patterns
d. R-controlled vowels.

100. First-grade students are given a sight-word list to practice for the week, containing the words below. Which word on the list contains a diphthong?

a. There
b. She
c. Tree
d. Boy

Constructed Response

1. Andrew is a first-grade student who is reading a new text for the first time during his guided-reading group. His teacher is completing a running record as he reads to determine which strategies he is using and which types of errors he is making. His running record is shown below.

Sam loved animals. He had a small, spotted puppy that he loved to play with and take for walks. He even taught his puppy some tricks, like how to roll over and shake. Sometimes, he even walked his neighbors' dogs too, just for fun. That was how much he loved animals.

One weekend, Sam's neighbor came running over to his house. Her dog Max had dug a hole under the fence in the backyard and escaped. She was very worried and wanted to know if Sam would help. "Of course," Sam said. "I'll be right there."

Sam knew just what to do. He came out of his house and called for Max in an excited, playful voice. Within seconds, Sam could hear the jingle of Max's collar and knew he was nearby. "Come here, Max! I have a treat for you!" Sam called.

Suddenly, Max darted around the corner and ran right up to Sam. "Good boy," Sam said, as he handed Max a treat. Sam had saved the day.

Key

Deletion	⬭	Repetition	←
Insertion	∧	Self-Correction	©
Short Pause	|	Substitution	then / there
Long Pause	||		

Using knowledge of decoding strategies (e.g., use of semantic, syntactic, and visual cues; use of word recognition strategies; self-monitoring) write a response in which you both:

- Identify one of Andrew's strengths related to decoding words.
- Identify one of Andrew's weaknesses related to decoding words.

Use evidence from Andrew's running record to support your answer.

2. Kaitlyn is a second-grade student who reads a traditional version of the story *Goldilocks and the Three Bears*. After reading, the teacher asks the student to list character traits to describe Goldilocks, using evidence from the story to support her answer. Kaitlyn's response is shown below.

Well, first, Goldilocks is a girl. I know that because I saw pictures of her in the book, and she is wearing a dress and has long braids. Also, I think Goldilocks is a girl's name. She also has blond hair. I know that because her name is Goldilocks, and it says in the story that she got her name from her long golden hair. So that's my second answer. I also think she is brave. She is brave because she goes into a house that doesn't belong to her. She didn't even know who lived there, and it turned out to be bears. I would never go into a stranger's house because it could be dangerous.

Using knowledge of character analysis, write a response in which you both:

- Identify one of Kaitlyn's strengths related to character analysis.
- Identify one of Kaitlyn's weaknesses related to character analysis.

Use evidence from Kaitlyn's response to support your answer.

Answer Key and Explanations for Test #1

Multiple Choice Questions

1. B: Automaticity refers to the ability to recognize printed words quickly and effortlessly. Because sight word practice helps increase the number of words students can recognize quickly and effortlessly, it builds automaticity. Sight words can be difficult to decode using typical phonics rules. Phonemic awareness and phonological awareness involve identifying and manipulating sounds rather than reading printed words.

2. D: Encoding is the process of translating sounds to print using knowledge of letter/sound relationships. The student is listening to each sound in the word *stop* and remembering which letter makes that sound before writing it on paper. Decoding involves using knowledge of letter/sound relationships to translate written words into speech. Blending and segmenting are both phonological awareness skills that involve manipulating spoken sounds. They do not involve identifying the letters that make the sounds.

3. A: The student is using both the picture in the book and his prior knowledge to make sense of the text, which demonstrates use of the semantic cueing system. When using the syntactic cueing system, readers select words that sound right using knowledge of grammar and sentence structure. When readers use the graphophonic cueing system, they use knowledge of letter/sound relationships to decode words. When using pragmatic cues, readers consider their purposes for reading in given situations.

4. C: Phonological awareness and phonemic awareness are distinct terms. Phonological awareness is a broader term that refers to the ability to identify and manipulate sounds in spoken words. Phonemic awareness is one component of phonological awareness involving the ability to identify and manipulate sounds in spoken words at the phoneme level. Because phonemes are the smallest units of speech, phonemic awareness is an advanced component of phonological awareness. It typically develops after simpler skills, like rhyming and blending.

5. D: Rhyming, or identifying words with the same ending sound, is typically considered to be the simplest phonological awareness skill. Children typically develop the ability to rhyme before developing more complex phonological awareness skills, including syllabification, segmenting onsets and rimes, and blending.

6. D: Prosody refers to reading with appropriate intonation, rhythm, and stress. Because Liz is reading in a monotone voice and not using appropriate phrasing, it would be beneficial for her teacher to focus on prosody during small-group instruction. Her accuracy rate is in the independent range, which demonstrates she has strong word recognition skills. Her high accuracy rate also suggests she is already reading with automaticity.

7. D: Phonemic awareness refers to the ability to identify and manipulate sounds at the phoneme level. Because phonemes are the smallest units of spoken sound, phonemic awareness is the most advanced phonological awareness skill.

8. B: By taking a whole word and breaking it into its individual sounds, the students are practicing segmenting. Blending is the opposite process, where students take individual sounds and combine them to form a whole word. Phoneme isolation refers to identifying the beginning, middle, or ending sound in a word. Phoneme identification refers to identifying a common sound in a group of words with either the same beginning, middle, or ending sound.

9. C: Phonological awareness skills typically progress in a similar manner. The ability to rhyme often develops first, as it is considered the simplest skill. Later, children develop the ability to break words into syllables, which is usually followed by the ability to manipulate onsets and rimes. Phoneme isolation and other phonemic awareness skills typically develop last, as they are the most complex.

10. B: Pointing to each word as it is read aloud will help students understand the relationship between the printed and spoken word. They will begin to understand that the meaning of the story is contained in the text. Showing students where to begin reading on each page and how to complete a return sweep will help them track the text appropriately. Asking students what they see in the pictures encourages the use of the semantic cueing system.

11. D: Phonemes are the smallest units of sound in words. In this activity, students are replacing one phoneme with another, which is known as phoneme substitution. Alliteration refers to a series of words in which most words begin with the same sound. Segmenting refers to breaking a word down into its individual sounds, or phonemes. Onset and rime blending involve blending the beginning sound of a word with the rest of the word.

12. A: Environmental print is the print people see in their everyday lives. For children, this may include restaurant logos, food labels, and street signs. Environmental print helps children understand that print has meaning, and reading familiar words can boost reading confidence. The remaining options provide students with opportunities to read other types of meaningful words, but not environmental print.

13. C: Readers use the syntactic cueing system when they consider sentence structure and grammar to decode unknown words. Alex is substituting a word that sounds right in the sentence. If Alex were using the graphophonic cueing system, he would choose a word that is structurally similar to the existing word, such as a word that starts with the same sound. If Alex were using the semantic cueing system, he would use picture cues or prior knowledge to guess the word. The pragmatic cueing system refers to consideration of the purposes of reading in given situations.

14. A: During interactive writing experiences, teachers and students work together to create writing pieces. Teachers and students share the writing utensils, with teachers guiding the students as they record their thoughts. In shared writing experiences, teachers record students' thoughts on paper. Students do not help with the writing. In independent writing, students utilize the strategies they have learned to complete writing pieces independently. Guided writing occurs when teachers work with small groups of strategically grouped students on targeted writing skills.

15. D: Portfolios are collections of students' writing samples gathered over time. Students can review their writing samples and use observations, checklists, or rubrics to evaluate how their writing skills have evolved over time. Norm-referenced and criterion-referenced tests are both formal and standardized tests. Norm-referenced tests compare students' performances to the performances of sample groups of similar students. Criterion-referenced tests indicate whether or not students have mastered certain skills and identify which skills require additional instruction. Students write for authentic purposes when completing performance-based tasks, but these do not show growth over time.

16. A: Concepts of print are conventions used to convey meaning in printed text. They include locating the title and author's name, holding the book correctly, tracking print, reading from left to right, and other similar concepts. Phonological awareness is the ability to identify and manipulate sounds in spoken words, and phonemic awareness is the ability to identify and manipulate sounds at the phoneme level. Close reading is a strategy where students deeply analyze texts to increase comprehension.

17. D: A story map helps students identify the main events of a fictional story, along with the conflict and resolution. Listing the main events can assist Michael with writing a concise summary. A KWL chart helps students identify what they know, want to know, and learned about a topic. A semantic map contains a word or concept in the center of a diagram, with related words or phrases branching off from the middle. It is useful for helping students identify relationships between concepts. A Venn diagram helps students compare and contrast two or more things.

18. A: It is beneficial for ELLs to practice phonemic awareness skills on words they know in English. Some English phonemes may not be used in students' native languages. Therefore, introducing English vocabulary words that contain these phonemes helps give these sounds a meaningful context. While phonological and phonemic awareness in students' native languages can be beneficial when they are learning English, it may lead to overgeneralization of rules of the native languages. Therefore, in instructional settings, using familiar words in English will help students practice the phonemes and patterns of English. Students will need to gradually learn phonemes that are not part of their native languages, but it is not ideal to introduce them first. Phonological and phonemic awareness assists with learning the alphabetic principle, so it is beneficial for students to develop these skills first.

19. D: Implicit phonics instruction uses a whole-to-part approach, with students reading whole texts rather than starting with isolated phonemes. Students learn to recognize whole words by sight. Through analyzing and comparing words, they then discover phonics and spelling patterns. A benefit is that students read authentic texts and learn in a meaningful context rather than practicing skills in isolation. However, research has shown that explicit phonics instruction, which progresses from part to whole, leads to stronger decoding, spelling, and comprehension skills.

20. B: Explicit phonics instruction uses a part-to-whole approach. Mr. Clark's students first learn the *st* blend in isolation before applying it to whole words. Implicit phonics instruction, also referred to as whole language or analytical phonics, uses a whole-to-part approach. Students recognize whole words by sight before breaking them down into individual phonemes.

21. C: Following the text with a pointer and pointing to each word with a finger both help with the concept of directionality. Directionality includes the understanding that you read from left to right, from top to bottom, and from the left page to the right page. Spacing refers to the understanding that you include spaces between words and between sentences. Book orientation refers to knowing how to hold and open a book correctly. Letter concepts include recognizing letters and knowing the difference between a letter and a word.

22. D: While all of these options can assist students with learning letter formation, writing letters in shaving cream best represents a multisensory approach. It involves movement, touch, and sight.

23. A: Alphabetic principle is the understanding that each letter of the alphabet makes a predictable sound. Students are practicing this by repeating the letter name and sound each week. Concepts of print are conventions used to convey meaning in text. Examples include knowing how to hold a book and track text correctly. Phonological awareness is the ability to identify and manipulate sounds in words. It does not involve letter/sound relationships. Automaticity refers to the ability to recognize whole words quickly and effortlessly.

24. B: R-controlled vowels appear before the letter *r* in a word. The *r* changes the sound of the vowel. In the other options, the *r* comes before the vowel, and the vowel sound is not changed.

25. D: A consonant digraph is a group of two or three consonants that form a new consonant sound when combined. The *ch* in the word *cheek* forms a new sound. The other choices contain consonant blends. In consonant blends, two or three consonants blend together, but each individual letter sound is still heard.

26. C: Word families are an effective strategy for teaching CVCe words. Once students have determined the sound made by the last three letters using knowledge of the silent *e* rule, they can identify other rhyming words within the same family by changing the first letter. This increases the number of words they can easily decode. Because these words have a silent letter that affects the vowel sound, covering parts of the word, chunking, and blending are not as effective.

27. A: Introducing new vocabulary words will help students decode the words faster when they are encountered in the text, thus assisting with fluency. Recognizing the words and knowing their meanings will also build readers' confidence. Additionally, explaining the meanings of the words in advance will help students comprehend the text when they read it independently. Reading the first few pages aloud without discussion will not help students recognize or understand the vocabulary words, nor will it highlight important words beyond the first few pages. Listing what students want to learn about the topic helps to set a purpose for reading, not explain vocabulary. Predicting helps students activate prior knowledge, make connections, and stay actively engaged in the reading process.

28. C: When students reread familiar texts, they do not need to exert energy on decoding unfamiliar words. As a result, more energy is available to focus on fluency, including phrasing and expression. Choral reading allows students to match their reading rate and expression with others in the group who are modeling fluent reading, including the teacher. Reading new texts requires students to spend more energy on decoding and comprehension, which may interfere with fluency. Audio versions of texts can serve as models of fluent reading, but students still need opportunities to practice. Partner reading may be helpful if students are matched with fluent readers, but this is not guaranteed.

29. B: Semantics is the branch of linguistics that deals with meaning. The semantic system in language includes all aspects of language use that carries meaning. Semantics include words, phrases, sentences, and further contexts that help to convey meaning. Semantics are involved in both receptive and expressive language processes. Choice A is incorrect because the graphophonic system is largely related to the sounds of a language and their written representations. Graphophonics study the relationship between phonics and orthography (writing system). Choice C is incorrect because the syntactic system refers primarily to sentence structure, word order, and other elements of grammar. Syntax does impact meaning, but in a more indirect way than semantics. Choice D is incorrect because pragmatics refers to practical application of language in a variety of contexts. For example, pragmatics is interested in language shifts between social and academic contexts. In reading, this involves being aware of how writers use language to convey moods and draw out more subtle implications.

30. C: Long before babies are able to speak, read, or write, they learn language skills by listening. Through listening, children learn rules of grammar, syntax, and pragmatics. They also develop their vocabularies.

31. D: When young children recognize environmental print, they learn that print contains meaning. For example, a child who recognizes a familiar fast-food sign understands that the words represent the restaurant name. Children often recognize environmental print before learning specific letter names and letter/sound relationships. Additionally, environmental print often contains complex spelling patterns and is difficult for beginning readers to decode. Environmental print does not teach one-to-one correspondence unless someone reads the print while simultaneously pointing to each individual word.

32. A: In shared writing experiences, students share thoughts during a class discussion, and the teacher records them on paper. Because students are in the preliterate stage of writing, they are not yet using sound/symbol relationships to spell words. Writing at this stage may resemble scribbling or contain strings of pretend letters. If Mr. Suarez records the students' thoughts for this activity, the story can be reread multiple times. If students write independently or with partners, it will be difficult to maintain the message of the story each time it is reread. Similar difficulties would occur with interactive writing because students help write the shared story on paper.

33. C: Picture walks are frequently used to activate students' prior knowledge. When readers look at the pictures, they make connections between the content of the new texts and what they already know from other texts or life experiences. These connections can spark interest in the stories and deepen comprehension. Teachers may encourage the use of syntactic cues during guided reading groups, but this is not typically part of a picture walk. Setting a purpose for reading is another beneficial prereading activity, but it is not always a part of a picture walk either. Metacognitive skills, which assist students with self-monitoring during reading, are also beneficial, but they are not typically the focus of a picture walk.

34. C: Word sorts assist students with comparing and contrasting features of words. While completing the sort, students must analyze each word to determine and categorize its vowel sound and determine how each word is similar to and different from other words in the set. Segmenting words using Elkonin boxes helps students break words into individual phonemes, but it doesn't assist with comparing and contrasting. Tracing words may help students practice short vowel spelling patterns, but it doesn't assist with comparing and contrasting either. Including words with short vowel sounds on the weekly spelling list will mainly assist with learning spelling patterns.

35. B: Explicit and systematic phonics instruction involves planning the teaching of specific phonics skills in a logical order, from simplest to most complex, using a part-to-whole approach. It requires understanding students' existing phonics knowledge and planning instruction to address specific skills that they still need to develop. Choice A and choice D demonstrate implicit phonics instruction, where students read whole texts, and phonics instruction occurs based on students' struggles and/or observations as they read. It uses a whole-to-part approach. Choice C involves preplanned phonics instruction, but the teacher is selecting phonics skills to address based on the content of the books rather than a research-based sequencing of skills from simplest to most complex.

36. D: Alphabetic principle is the understanding that each letter makes a predictable sound. Students are practicing the alphabetic principle by matching the letter to a word that begins with the sound that letter makes. Encoding is the process of translating phonemes to graphemes, or recording sounds using letters. One-to-one correspondence is the understanding that each printed word corresponds with one spoken word. Phoneme isolation is the identification of the beginning, middle, or ending sound in a word.

37. B: When students combine the initial sound in a word with the remainder of the word, they are blending the onset and rime. Syllabification involves breaking a word into syllables. A word may have one or more syllables. Phoneme isolation involves identifying either the beginning, middle, or ending sound in a word. Segmentation involves breaking a word into its individual sounds.

38. C: While all of these activities can positively contribute to children's language and literacy development over time, children begin language development through listening. Talking and singing to babies from the time of birth contributes to language development. Around the age of two, they begin to develop early phonological awareness skills, such as rhyming. They also gradually begin to recognize environmental and other types of print.

39. C: Decoding, fluency, and comprehension are interrelated. The student is likely spending a lot of mental energy trying to decode unknown words, leaving little energy left to focus on comprehension. Additionally, repeatedly stopping to decode words interrupts fluency. This may cause the reader to struggle to make connections between the disjointed words and sentences. Implicit phonics instruction is not the best intervention option, as research has shown that systematic and explicit phonics instruction is most effective. Additionally, there is not enough information available to determine the cause of the student's decoding difficulties. Therefore, it cannot be assumed that it is related to a lack of phonological awareness skills or a language processing disorder.

40. D: Multisyllabic words often contain smaller parts that students recognize, such as prefixes, roots, and suffixes. Identifying these known parts can help students figure out the words. Context clues can help students guess words that make sense, but students should be able to apply word analysis skills to cross check their guesses and ensure they are selecting the correct words. Stretching out the sounds and blending the phonemes are helpful strategies for decoding shorter words with predictable spelling patterns. However, these strategies are less reliable for decoding multisyllabic words with more complex spelling patterns.

41. A: A morpheme is the smallest unit of language with meaning. An example is the prefix *pre*, which means before. *Pre* cannot be broken down any further without losing its meaning. The smallest unit of speech is a phoneme. A grapheme is a letter or group of letters representing a single sound. A syllable is a unit of spoken language in a word that contains a single uninterrupted sound.

42. C: The words *won* and *one* are homophones because they sound the same, but are spelled differently and have different meanings. The words *multitask* and *multiple* in choice A have the same prefix. Choice B contains a homograph pair with the words *park* (to leave your car in a location) and *park* (an outside recreational area). These words are spelled the same, but they have different meanings. Choice D contains rhyming words, *bees* and *trees.*

43. D: A prefix is a letter or group of letters added to the beginning of a word that changes the meaning of the word. *Mis* is a prefix meaning *wrong*. When added to the word *lead*, a new word, *mislead*, is formed. This new word means to lead in the wrong manner, or deceive. *Mis* does not act as a prefix in the word *mist* because it is not added to a word to change the meaning. Without the *mis,* only the letter *t* remains. *Cooking* contains a suffix, or a letter or group of letters added to the end of a word. *Trap* does not contain any prefixes or suffixes.

44. B: Semantic maps are used to create visual representations of connections between items. Students can put the root in the middle of the semantic map and display words containing the root on the branches, thus demonstrating what the words have in common. Looking up words in the dictionary or finding them in the textbook does not facilitate making connections unless follow-up discussions or activities occur. While Venn diagrams are used to compare and contrast two or more things, the web-like format of the semantic map better displays the connections between related words.

45. A: The focus of this activity is on comparing the meanings of the words before and after the suffix *less* is added. Students should recognize that the newly formed words mean *without* (base word) and be able to apply this knowledge to figure out the meanings of other words containing the same suffix. While students may also learn to spell and decode words containing *less* as a result of this activity, the primary focus is on the words' meanings. Choice D is incorrect because *less* is a suffix. Prefixes are letters or groups of letters added to the beginnings of words.

46. B: Homographs are words that are spelled the same way but have different meanings. For example, *minute* (the unit of time) and *minute* (tiny), are homographs. Note that homographs can also be pronounced differently. Words that are spelled differently but pronounced the same way are called homophones. Words with the same Latin root or words within the same word family are related to one another, but they are not homographs.

47. D: Chunking involves looking for known parts in a word. Because *scapegoat* is a compound word, it is likely that Maria will at least recognize the word *goat*. This leaves a smaller portion of the word to decode. There are many words that would sound right in the sentence, so guessing based on syntax alone is unlikely to result in the correct word. Because the word is multisyllabic and contains multiple spelling patterns, blending may be difficult. Additionally, the sentence provides few context clues to help Maria guess the word correctly.

48. C: This sentence contains the word *firm*, which is an antonym for *tentative*. This antonym, along with the word *unlike*, help the reader determine that *tentative* means not firm. There are no synonyms, or words that mean the same, for *tentative* in the sentence. There are also no definitions for the word. Inference clues give hints about the word's meaning without explicitly listing a synonym, antonym, or definition. No such inference clues are present.

49. A: Cognates are words in different languages that share the same roots, such as the English word *conflict* and the Spanish word *conflicto*. If students know the meanings of the words in their native languages, they can apply that knowledge to determine the meanings of the English words. Realia are everyday objects that provide visual representations of words, also contributing to vocabulary development. While recognizing known parts in cognates can assist students with decoding new words quickly, it is less likely to assist with prosody. Phonological and phonemic awareness have to do with identifying and manipulating sounds in words rather than identifying word meanings or related spelling patterns.

50. A: An idiom is a type of figurative language in which the entire phrase has a unique meaning that cannot be determined from the meanings of the individual words. This idiom means that it is raining very hard, which does not match the literal meaning of the phrase. Proverbs are short, well-known sayings that offer wisdom or advice. A simile is a figure of speech used to compare two things using *like* or *as*. A metaphor is a figure of speech used to compare two things without the use of *like* or *as*.

51. A: Tier-two vocabulary words are high-frequency and challenging words that hold a lot of meaning within the text. Because they appear frequently, not knowing their meanings can affect comprehension in multiple texts. High-frequency, concrete nouns are tier-one words. These are usually learned through everyday interactions and do not require explicit instruction. Domain-specific words are tier-three words. While it is beneficial for students to learn and use these words in some academic and professional contexts, they are unlikely to appear in everyday texts. Student-selected words may be used to generate interest in the topic and help students become actively involved in their learning. However, there is no guarantee that students will choose high-frequency words.

52. B: Metacognition refers to thinking about one's own thinking. Proficient readers use metacognitive skills to self-monitor their own understanding and make corrections when necessary. Making predictions, and then later assessing and revising them if necessary, demonstrates use of metacognitive skills. The other options require students to recall and/or analyze information, but they do not ask students to reflect on their own thinking.

53. A: Venn diagrams consist of overlapping circles, which visually represent the similarities and differences between two or more items. They are commonly used for compare and contrast activities. Story maps are used to identify the components of fictional stories, such as the characters and setting. Five W's charts are used to identify details in stories by answering who, what, where, when, and why questions. T-charts allow students to contrast two items, but there is no visual representation of the similarities between them.

54. D: Pragmatics refers to understanding the social rules of communication, including the ability to adjust the level of formality to match a specific social situation. Morphology refers to understanding word parts and word forms. Semantics refers to understanding the meanings of words. Syntax refers to understanding grammar and sentence structure.

55. C: Close reading involves multiple readings of the same text, with students analyzing different layers of the text each time. Students read the texts independently, with no picture walks or pre-teaching beforehand. Close reading is designed to help students become actively involved in the reading process and develop deeper understandings of what they have read. Guided reading is done in small groups, with teachers focusing on targeted skills based on students' needs. Additionally, picture walks are often done in guided reading groups. SQ3R is a strategy often used to help students comprehend textbook readings. It involves students doing a quick survey of the text, followed by identification of questions about the text. Students then read the text, recite it in their own words, and review the main idea. Scanning involves reading quickly to identify specific information.

56. B: Literal comprehension is an understanding of what is actually stated in the text by the author. Questions of this type involve recalling information and often answer who, what, when, where, or why. Affective comprehension refers to readers' personal reactions to texts based on their individual experiences, prior knowledge, and preferences. Inferential comprehension is a deeper level of comprehension than literal comprehension. It requires readers to make inferences when the answers to questions are not directly stated in the text. Evaluative comprehension is a deeper level than both literal and inferential comprehension. It involves using prior knowledge and textual evidence to form judgments about the text.

57. A: Evaluative questions require readers to form opinions or judgements based on the text. Asking if readers agree with something the author stated is an evaluative question. The remaining questions ask students to recall information only.

58. B: The keywords in choice B are used to signal how two or more items are the same and different, which is the purpose of compare-and-contrast texts. The keywords in choice A would likely be found in descriptive texts. The keywords in choice C would likely be found in cause-and-effect texts. The keywords in choice D would likely be found in sequential texts.

59. D: Synthesis involves gathering information from multiple sources and combining it to make meaning, as students are doing when they write their research reports on sustainable farming practices. As students collect information from each source, they also consider how their initial thoughts on the topic have changed. Evaluating involves making a judgment about something. Inferring involves using clues in the text to make meaning rather than using information that is directly stated. Drawing conclusions involves making judgements based on inferences.

60. C: When students make text-to-self connections, they make connections between the texts and their own personal experiences. This student connects Alicia's experiences adjusting to a new situation to her own adjustment when moving to a new school. Choice A demonstrates a text-to-text connection, when students make connections between two or more different texts they have read. Choice B demonstrates a text-to-world connection, when students make connections between texts and events that have happened in the real world, but not to themselves personally. Choice D represents a student's reaction to the book rather than a connection between two or more things.

61. B: Aidan is writing to convince the cafeteria manager to act on a specific request, and he supports his request with reasons. This is indicative of persuasive writing. When authors write to inform, they share information about their topics to teach readers new things. When authors write to entertain, they write to provide readers with enjoyable experiences. When authors write to describe, they write to share descriptive details about their topics.

62. B: The best model a teacher can provide to students in this situation is effective reading strategies that result in better overall comprehension. Choice B effectively accomplishes this by first reading for the main idea, which is easier to grasp than smaller details that can be misleading or unrelated to the point of the passage. Reading, then re-reading is a great skill to show students to help them know to approach the text and be willing to put more time in to understand the passage more fully, rather than just looking for information for a particular answer. Choice A is wrong because while learning to underline meaningful information in a passage is useful, going straight to the place where the answers are located does not help model the overall search for information. Choice C is wrong because it pertains to general test-taking tips and is not directly related to reading comprehension or use of textual evidence. Choice D is wrong because it models weak practices. It is generally not a good idea to complete an organizational framework until you are well-acquainted with a passage. The whole text should be read first, then when the overall idea is understood, someone can go back and fill in a story map.

63. B: Sensory charts are used to gather details about a topic using the five senses. They are helpful for planning descriptive essays, as these details describe what the topic looks like, sounds like, smells like, tastes like, or feels like. These descriptive details can help the reader to imagine the topic of the essay in greater detail. Sequencing charts are helpful for essays that use a time-order text structure. T-charts are useful for planning essays that use a comparative text structure. Persuasive maps are useful for planning persuasive essays, as they help the writers plan which details they will use to support their topics.

64. B: If students read two versions of the same fairy tale narrated by two different characters, they can contrast the versions of events that are described and discuss how each character's situations and feelings may affect the way the story is told. Choice A and choice C allow students to respond individually to the story, but they do not offer students the opportunity to compare situations from two different points of view. Choice D helps students compare and contrast two sets of events, but it also does not address two different points of view.

65. A: Spoken language is generally less formal and more conversational in tone than written language. As a result, syntax is more relaxed, and there is greater flexibility in word order. Spoken language also tends to contain a mixture of sentences and fragments. For example, a typical conversation among friends may contain several shifts between speakers, along with brief comments and replies rather than fully developed sentences. Body language plays a greater role in spoken language, as it can either affirm or contradict the meaning of the spoken words. For example, if a person says they are looking forward to something, yet they are frowning and avoiding eye contact, the recipient of the message may not believe the speaker is sincere.

66. D: When readers visualize, they use the clues and details in the stories to form mental pictures in their minds. When students draw a setting based on how they imagined it from the description in the story, they are visualizing. Predicting refers to making guesses about the text before reading. Inferring refers to using clues in the story to determine the meaning when it is not explicitly stated. Summarizing refers to retelling the main events of the story.

67. C: Using context clues can help the reader determine the meanings of many unknown words quickly and also contribute to reading comprehension. Asking a classmate for the meanings of words may work in the short term, but it does not help the reader develop independent reading strategies, and there may not always be another person present while reading. Looking up the unknown words later may result in the student missing words that are critical to the meaning of the text, negatively affecting comprehension. Similarly, while skipping over the unknown words may result in sentences that appear to make sense, the missing words may play important roles in the meaning.

68. C: Daniel has identified only external character traits, or traits related to the character's appearance. He has not identified any internal traits, or traits related to the character's thoughts, feelings, words, or actions. An appropriate next step would be to help Daniel differentiate between the two types of traits and find examples of each in the text. The remaining options would require Daniel to identify internal traits using textual evidence. For example, it would be difficult to describe how the character has changed throughout the story without using any internal traits to describe her at different points in the story. Similarly, it would be difficult to label the role she plays or compare her with other characters without using any internal traits to support the responses.

69. D: Meg is creating an expository research report to share information about the costs involved in pet ownership. The information she obtained from the website contains opinions rather than facts, which is signaled using phrases like "I believe" and "most loyal." It is important for Meg to differentiate between the two so that she can support her topic with facts. While Meg will likely need to synthesize information from multiple sources, choose an appropriate text structure, and include text features, the information provided indicates that differentiating between facts and opinions is an immediate need in order for Meg to successfully complete the assignment.

70. C: Although the names of the stages vary, readers generally progress through four stages of reading development: emergent reading, early reading, transitional reading, and fluent reading. The name "transitional phase" refers to the transition from having to learn to read to being able to read to learn. The greatest need for students in the transitional phase is to be able to navigate unfamiliar words in passages. To do so, they need to be able to use morphology (C), such as prefixes, suffixes, and parts of speech, to help determine the meaning of newly-encountered words. Students in the transitional stage should already have many sight words memorized (A) and have letter/sound correspondence (D) nearly mastered. Identifying themes in abstract texts (B) is probably beyond the capability of students in the transitional stage.

71. A: Emergent readers are learning concepts of print, and they benefit from having text in familiar places to assist with tracking and directionality. They are still developing phonics skills and may rely on one or more cueing systems, so picture support is important for determining unknown words. Emergent readers also benefit from simple sentence structure and repetition, which assists them with guessing unknown words. The features in choice B are more appropriate for early readers who are beginning to read more complex texts and are able to use phonics skills and multiple cueing systems rather than relying on picture clues. The features in choice C are more appropriate for transitional readers who are able to read a wider range of genres and text structures independently. Choice D is appropriate for fluent readers who are able to read complex, technical, and abstract texts independently.

72. A: When readers skim, they look through a text quickly to determine what it is mostly about. Skimming would help the students quickly identify which sites listed in the search results are closely related to the science fair topics and warrant further, deeper reading. Scanning involves reading quickly to pick out certain pieces of information from a text, such as a specific fact or date. Close reading involves rereading a text multiple times while analyzing different layers each time. Extensive reading refers to students selecting books that are enjoyable and easy to read independently, which helps increase reading rate and fluency.

73. B: Generally, a book that is read with 90-94% accuracy is considered within the student's instructional reading level. This is the level at which the text presents some challenges that can lead to growth, while not being so difficult as to cause frustration. Texts read with less than 90% accuracy are considered to be at the frustration level, and are too difficult for students to read without becoming discouraged. Texts read with 95% accuracy or greater are considered to be at the independent reading level. These are texts that students can easily read without assistance. They are good options for free-choice reading time and other purposes, but are not ideal candidates for guided reading instruction because they are not challenging enough to lead to growth. Lexile levels refer to a system for leveling books.

74. D: Research indicates that frequent guided reading using texts in students' instructional reading levels best supports reading development. Reading texts that are challenging but not frustrating helps students learn new strategies and vocabulary while receiving targeted instruction specific to their needs. Because students' needs can change quickly as they develop new skills, it is important for these groups to be flexible in nature. Choices A and B are incorrect because the same text will not be in the instructional level for all students. Choice C is incorrect because students should be assessed and regrouped frequently, not only quarterly.

75. D: Charlie did not acknowledge any errors, but instead kept reading after each one. Proficient readers recognize when something does not look right, sound right, or make sense, and they try again until they find the correct words. The teacher can prompt Charlie to stop and question himself when he makes errors until he begins recognizing and self-correcting them on his own. Because Charlie's errors both make sense and sound right in the sentences, he is already using both semantic and syntactic cues. The student only omitted one minor word, which did not change the meaning of the sentence.

76. A: A test is valid if it measures what it is designed to measure. If a test claims to measure a student's ability to make inferences, then the questions on the test should require students to use this skill. Reliability refers to ensuring that there is consistency in test results over time and between participants. Bias refers to ensuring that the test does not put any participants at a disadvantage. Objectivity refers to ensuring that all tests are scored in the same manner without being affected by any outside influences or bias.

77. C: Constructivism is a learning theory based on the idea that people are actively involved in the learning process, rather than being passive receivers of knowledge. Constructivism suggests that children learn best by solving real-world problems, gathering information, testing ideas, and other active processes, with teachers guiding and scaffolding them along the way.

78. A: According to Vygotsky, activities in the zone of proximal development are ones that students are almost able to complete independently, but they require some scaffolding. The activities are not too easy or too difficult, but just challenging enough to allow some growth to occur. Reading books at the instructional level with teacher guidance is an example of an activity in the zone of proximal development. Choices B and D represent activities that are easy for the student. Choice C demonstrates a way to make a text accessible for a student when it is too difficult for the student to read independently.

79. C: Accommodation occurs when something challenges a person's existing schema and causes it to be altered. In choice C, the child has a negative opinion of bees until she learns the role that they play in pollination. Her schema is altered, and she now views them as helpful. The other options demonstrate examples of assimilation, which occurs when someone takes in new information and adds it to existing schema rather than changing it. In choice A, the student applies the information she knows about sentences to punctuate the question. In choice B, the student applies information about the writing process to a new type of text. In choice D, the child assumes that the tiger is a lion because it makes the same sound.

80. B: Schemata are units of existing knowledge used to make sense of newly encountered information. Readers rely on their existing schemata to make sense of information encountered in new texts. Therefore, activating prior knowledge is a key component of schema theory. For example, a child may know that flowers require water to grow. He may use this existing schema to make sense of a new text about the desert, which indicates that few plants grow there. Summarizing, identifying main idea, and recognizing story elements all require finding key information within a text, but they do not necessarily relate this information to what was already known about the topic prior to reading.

81. B: When children reach the preoperational stage, they begin to think symbolically. At this point, they are able to begin understanding the relationship between letters (symbols) and sounds, also known as the alphabetic principle. Children are typically in the sensorimotor stage until about age 2, and they are not yet able to think symbolically in this stage. The concrete operational stage lasts from ages 7 to 12, and the formal operational stage lasts from age 12 until adulthood.

82. C: Cognitivism suggests that new information should be broken up into manageable chunks with ample opportunities for practice and feedback if learning is to occur. Presenting too much information at one time can result in cognitive overload. Choice A represents social learning theory, which highlights the importance of social interactions in learning. Choice B represents behaviorism, which focuses on the role that reinforcement plays in the continuance of certain behaviors. Choice D represents constructivism, which highlights the role of students being actively involved in the learning process.

83. D: Scaffolding occurs when teachers provide assistance to help students accomplish tasks that they are almost able to complete independently. In this example, the teacher introduces words that may be challenging to students to enable them to read the text independently. Choice A does not specify what role, if any, the teacher will play in assisting students with the building challenge, so no scaffolding is demonstrated. In choice B, the teacher is reading a book that is too difficult for students to read independently, meaning the task is out of students' zone of proximal development. Choice C represents an independent activity that students complete without any assistance.

84. B: Choice B best represents constructivism because students are using reading, writing, listening, and speaking skills to perform an authentic task that they collaboratively agreed upon. The teacher acts as a guide to facilitate the process. While students are engaged in higher-level thinking activities during the close reading activity in choice A, the activity is planned and led by the teacher. Similarly, the order and content of the stations in choice C have been determined by the teacher, and the activities do not represent authentic, performance-based tasks. Choice D, while providing beneficial modeling and social learning interaction, does not include students performing authentic, problem-based tasks.

85. A: A key tenet of Marie Clay's theory is the understanding that children take different paths to becoming readers based on differences in prior knowledge and experiences. As a result, teachers must meet the needs of individual learners rather than using a one-size-fits-all approach to instruction. Choice B is incorrect because Clay's theory also explains the interrelationship between reading and writing. Choice C is incorrect because Clay's theory emphasizes the importance of individualized instruction based on students' unique needs and experiences. Choice D is incorrect because frequent observation and data collection are important components of individualized instruction, as they allow teachers to determine students' strengths and needs.

86. C: Bias occurs when a test disadvantages a certain group of students. Including questions with cultural references that only a select group of students will understand disadvantages other students who do not understand the references. Students may miss these questions, despite having the reading skills the test is supposed to measure. Validity refers to whether the test measures what it is supposed to measure. Reliability relates to consistency of the test results over time and between participants.

87. A: Rubrics are a type of evaluation tool that assign both overall scores and scores in individual component areas of an assignment. In each component area, the criteria used to assign scores for different levels of mastery are outlined. Therefore, students can see their overall grades on assignments, as well as how they performed in each component area. This helps students assess their strengths and weaknesses. Rubrics do not specifically track progress over time, though teachers could evaluate students using the same rubric at different points of the year and compare the results. Rubrics assess individual performance and do not compare students to their peers. Choice D describes a miscue analysis, which is a different type of assessment.

88. D: Informal Reading Inventories assess students in multiple areas of reading performance, including decoding, comprehension, recall, and fluency. The results can be used to identify areas in need of improvement, group students for targeted reading instruction, and match students with appropriate texts. They do not record texts students have read throughout the year, which can be done using reading logs, nor do they identify areas of student interest. Other assessment and screening tools exist to determine which reading behaviors and skills students have already learned prior to entering school.

89. C: Research has shown that reading and writing are interrelated processes, and literacy development is enhanced when they are taught together. Even very young children can be encouraged to use writing to communicate, though their early attempts at writing may be scribbles. This helps children develop an understanding that print carries meaning, and it also assists with development of directionality and other concepts of print. Similarly, children learn concepts of print and skills that they use in their writing by seeing them modeled in the books they read.

90. A: Formative assessments are given during a unit of study to identify students' existing knowledge and gaps. They are used to guide instruction by helping a teacher determine if current instructional strategies are successful or if changes need to be made. Summative assessments are given at the end of a unit or after another extended period of time. Norm-referenced tests are standardized tests that compare students' performances to sample groups of similar students. Screening assessments are used to identify students who may be at risk for future academic difficulties and may benefit from interventions.

91. B: Choice B requires the highest level of thinking out of these options because it requires students to evaluate the author's craft. Comparing, contrasting, and inferring are in the comprehension level, which is lower. Identifying the setting is at the knowledge level of Bloom's taxonomy, which is the lowest level.

92. C: Writing their own examples of metaphors requires students to apply their knowledge. Identifying and underlining metaphors assesses the comprehension level of Bloom's taxonomy, and defining a metaphor assesses the knowledge level. Critiquing the author's use of metaphors assesses the evaluation level.

93. C: Semantics primarily refers to word meaning, often with a focus on the individual word, but sometimes including sentence and paragraph context. Any aspect of language that is used to convey meaning can technically considered a semantic property of language. Grammar, word order, and sentence structure are all aspects of syntax.

94. C: Text features are one factor used to level books. They help determine how much support readers have in decoding and comprehending the text. For example, pictures are one text feature essential for early readers. Other text features, such as headings and labels, can assist readers with expository texts. Therefore, text features are considered when leveling books. Considering both the author's purpose and craft can help students comprehend texts, but they do not typically affect leveling. Interest level will vary from student to student and is also not typically considered when leveling books.

95. D: When completing a running record, a teacher records the number of words the student reads correctly out of the total number of words in the text. This is used to calculate the accuracy rate, which helps to determine if the text is at the student's frustration, instructional, or independent reading level. Authentic assessment tasks provide opportunities for students to complete reading and writing activities while solving real-world problems rather than opportunities to calculate the accuracy rate when reading a text. Rubrics are used to evaluate students' performances based on multiple criteria on assignments and assessments, but they are not used to calculate accuracy rate, either. Guided reading observations may help the teacher determine if a text is much too easy or much too difficult for a student to read independently, but without the running record, the exact accuracy rate cannot be determined.

96. B: Informal assessments can consist of everyday activities, such as grading homework, observing students, taking anecdotal records, and talking to students about their learning. Therefore, the results are not standardized, making it difficult to compare results among groups or over time. The other options describe limitations of formal assessments, which may increase student anxiety and can be more expensive and time consuming to implement and score.

97. C: Formal assessments are administered and scored in a standardized fashion, so scoring is objective. Therefore, a standardized state reading test is an example of a formal reading assessment because all students take the test under the same conditions, and the tests should all be scored in the same way. The remaining options are situation dependent and not administered in a standardized manner. Additionally, various teachers may evaluate students differently, with results therefore being subjective.

98. D: Summative assessments are used to evaluate students' learning at the end of a unit, semester, school year, or other extended period of time. The remaining options describe formative assessments, which are given throughout the learning process and used to plan or adapt instruction during the unit based on students' performances.

99. C: Timothy made several mistakes when spelling long vowel sounds, using the CVCe spelling pattern for words that have two vowels in the middle. Because he made multiple errors with this spelling pattern and it can be applied to many other common words, it would be beneficial for the teacher to focus on this skill first. Although Timothy spelled *Tuesday* incorrectly, it is a more complex word that will likely take time and repetition to learn. He also will not be able to generalize that skill to spell many other words. He spelled the words with r-controlled vowels, *wore* and *car,* correctly.

100. D: A diphthong is formed when two vowel sounds are combined within a syllable, as with the /o/ and /y/ sounds in *boy*. Choices A and B contain consonant digraphs at the beginning. Choice C contains a consonant blend.

Constructed Response

1. Sample Response:

Andrew is showing a combination of strengths and weaknesses regarding his use of decoding strategies. His main strength is his use of graphophonic, or visual cues, to assist with decoding unknown words. However, a major weakness is that he is not consistently cross-checking his word choices with semantic or syntactic cues to ensure that his guesses make sense and sound right in the sentences.

When he comes to an unknown word, Andrew often looks at the first few letters and guesses a word that begins with those letters. For example, he said *field* for *fence*, *home* for *house*, *wondered* for *worried*, and *danced* for *darted*. This shows his use of visual, or graphophonic cues, though he concentrates on the beginning letters only. His use of visual cues would be enhanced if he looked at the middle and ending letters in the words in addition to the beginning letters.

Andrew's main weakness is that he does not stop to ask himself if these visual guesses make sense or sound right in the sentences. For example, he read "she was very *wondered*" instead of "she was very *worried*." While *wondered* and *worried* begin with the same two letters, *wondered* does not make sense or sound right in the sentence. However, Andrew continued reading without noticing his error. In another example, he read "*danced* around" instead of "*darted* around." While this sounds right, it does not make sense because Max is a dog. Andrew is therefore not consistently cross-checking his visual cues with semantic cues and syntactic cues, causing his errors to go unnoticed and uncorrected.

2. Sample Response:

Kaitlyn's response shows some strengths and weaknesses regarding character analysis. She uses text evidence and personal connections to support her choices, yet her selection of traits represents a mostly superficial analysis.

One of Kaitlyn's strengths is that she uses text evidence and personal connections to support her choice of character traits. She describes knowing that Goldilocks has long blond hair because the story described how she was named after a description of her hair. She supports her description of Goldilocks being a girl with clues she obtained from the picture support in the story, noting that she saw Goldilocks' dress and long braids. Additionally, she supports her decision to describe the character as brave by saying Goldilocks did not know who lived in the house when she entered it, and she herself would never enter a stranger's house because it could be dangerous. This indicates a personal connection and Kaitlyn's ability to use prior knowledge to influence her choices.

However, describing Goldilocks as a girl with long blond hair indicates a mostly superficial analysis. These are external character traits, or things you can tell just by looking at the character. Internal traits, or traits based on the character's thoughts, beliefs, or actions, are needed for a deeper analysis. Describing Goldilocks as brave was the only internal character trait mentioned. Therefore, Kaitlyn would need to select two more internal character traits for Goldilocks and support them by citing specific thoughts, beliefs, or actions described in the story to demonstrate a deeper level of understanding and analysis.

Practice Test #2

Multiple Choice Questions

1. As part of a poem she is writing, Isabella includes the following line:

"The river danced across the prairie, twirling and swirling in its path."

Which literary device is Isabella using in this line of her poem?

a. Simile
b. Personification
c. Onomatopoeia
d. Hyperbole

2. A student writes a fictional story about a man who struggles to work for a difficult boss. He includes the following sentences in the story:

"John never knew which boss he would meet in the office each morning. Would it be Dr. Jekyll or Mr. Hyde?"

Which type of literary device is the student using in this example?

a. Foreshadowing
b. Irony
c. Allusion
d. Pun

3. Fourth-grade students in Mr. Lee's class are writing persuasive speeches on topics of their choice and presenting them to the class. One student, Caleb, gives a speech regarding the types of foods the school cafeteria should serve. He states, "The cafeteria should stop serving meatloaf because nobody likes it." After the speech, Mr. Lee asks Caleb what research he conducted to arrive at that conclusion. Caleb responds by saying, "Nobody at my lunch table ever eats it. They just end up throwing it away at the end of lunch." Which type of faulty reasoning should Mr. Lee address with Caleb?

a. Illogical conclusion
b. Overgeneralization
c. Personal bias
d. Circular reasoning

4. A kindergarten teacher asks students to say the word *cart*. She then tells students to take away the /t/ sound and tell her what they get. Which type of phonemic awareness activity are students practicing?

a. Onset and rime manipulation
b. Segmenting
c. Phoneme isolation
d. Phoneme deletion

5. Which of the following activities best demonstrates a phonics activity?

a. Sorting rhyming words
b. Playing alphabet bingo and covering a letter when the teacher says its name
c. Matching picture cards to the consonant blends they begin with
d. Listening to a fictional story read aloud by the teacher and identifying the setting

6. A student is reading a fictional book and has difficulty decoding the word *maple*. Which spelling pattern could the teacher explain to help the student decode this word and similar words in the future?

a. Vowel digraph pairs
b. R-controlled vowels
c. Closed syllables
d. Open syllables

7. Research has indicated that which of the following options is the best predictor of early reading success?

a. Phonemic awareness
b. Interest in reading
c. Concepts of print
d. Oral vocabulary

8. A fourth-grade teacher wants to help his students analyze word morphology in order to identify the meanings of unknown words. Which word could he use to best exemplify the strategy of analyzing word morphology?

a. Trees
b. Manuscript
c. Butterfly
d. Ceiling

9. Which of the following activities would best help to create a classroom environment that promotes a love of reading for kindergarten students?

a. Going on a word hunt to locate words starting with a specific letter
b. Tracing sight words using stencils
c. Practicing phonics skills on the classroom computer
d. Reading a favorite rhyming text aloud together and discussing favorite parts

10. The words *classify*, *measure*, and *observe* are examples of what?

a. Listening vocabulary
b. Academic vocabulary
c. Receptive vocabulary
d. Expressive vocabulary

11. A teacher gives students the following set of words: *compare*, *organism*, *predict*, *cell*, *habitat*, and *conclude*. Students are instructed to sort the words into two categories. What is the primary purpose of this activity?

a. Classifying words according to morphology
b. Recognizing common spelling patterns used to decode words
c. Differentiating between academic and content vocabulary
d. Grouping words with similar meanings

12. Reader's theater can best assist students in which area?

a. Memorization of text
b. Reading fluency
c. Artistic development through prop creation
d. Creative writing

13. Mr. Bennet's fourth-grade students are practicing digital literacy skills as part of a math unit on financial literacy. They will be completing two digital assignments during this unit. One assignment is to write a blog post on budgeting that will be published on the school website. Another assignment is to write an email to a friend describing something they are saving up to buy. Which topic would be most beneficial for Mr. Bennet to teach to assist students with successfully completing both of these assignments?

a. Verifying online sources
b. Selecting relevant search keywords
c. Navigating nonlinear writing and hyperlinks in digital texts
d. Adjusting formality of language based on audience

14. Which of the following activities would be most developmentally appropriate to include in a prekindergarten reading center?

a. A consonant blend word sort
b. Word cards that students can sequence to form sentences
c. Letter outlines for students to fill in with beans
d. Compound word puzzles

Refer to the following for question 15:

Ms. Baird assigns students a historical fiction short story to read. She wants to check her students' individual comprehension skills, specifically their ability to support an idea with evidence from the text. However, one student appears to be struggling with the story. Ms. Baird gives this student a graphic organizer containing the following sentence stems: *Someone, Wanted, But, So, Then.*

15. The graphic organizer given to the struggling student would best help the student with which skill?

a. Inferring
b. Summarizing
c. Drawing conclusions
d. Evaluating

Refer to the following for question 16:

A third-grade science teacher gives her students one hour to read an article about penguins, take notes on important information, and use the notes to write a three-paragraph expository essay. Before they begin, the teacher writes the words *Spheniscidae, plumage,* and *Aptenodytes forsteri* on the board. She explains the meaning of each word. At the end of the hour, one student, Joshua, only has his notes completed. The teacher examines his notes, part of which are shown below.

> Penguins are animals that live in the Southern Hemisphere.
> Many people believe that penguins live in the Arctic, but that is not true.
> Penguins in Antarctica huddle together to stay warm. They take turns standing on the outside of the huddle, where it is colder.
> Penguins' feathers help protect them from the water and cold air.
> Penguins live in groups called colonies.

16. Which strategy would be most helpful for the teacher to focus on with Joshua to prepare him for similar tasks?

a. Grouping the notes into three sections to correspond with the paragraphs of the essay
b. Selecting only a few facts to record before moving on to the essay
c. Using drawings rather than words
d. Recording only key words and phrases rather than sentences

17. While reading an expository text aloud to students, a teacher makes the following comments.

"'The cheetah can accelerate to its top speed in about three seconds.' Hmm, I'm not sure what accelerate means. Let me read that again to see if the sentence has any clues. 'The cheetah can accelerate to its top speed in about three seconds.' It has something to do with the cheetah getting faster, so I think accelerate means to speed up."

What is the teacher demonstrating in this activity?

a. Forming mental images
b. Making a prediction
c. Thinking aloud
d. Visualizing

18. Laura is reading an expository text and struggles to decode the words *rabbit* and *problem*. Which spelling pattern would be most beneficial for the teacher to practice with Laura?

a. Open syllables
b. Closed syllables
c. CVCC spelling patterns
d. Double consonants

19. A second-grade teacher is designing a word sort to help her students identify inflectional endings. Which pair of words should she use in this activity?

a. Jumped and eating
b. *Blew* and *boo*
c. Crunch and trash
d. *Day* and *weigh*

20. Which of the following examples demonstrate students using a combination of digital and print-based media?

a. Students put sentence strips in order to retell the main events of a story they read in their reading textbook.
b. Students watch an animated story on an educational website and complete the accompanying online comprehension questions.
c. Students listen as their teacher reads a big book on plants aloud. Then they create a computer slideshow showing the stages of plant growth.
d. Students use free software to create a digital storyboard. Then they film a movie using the storyboard as a guide.

21. An ELL is having difficulties comprehending a science textbook because it contains many unknown vocabulary words with few accompanying visuals. Which instructional strategy would most likely assist the student with this difficulty?

a. Reading the textbook aloud to him rather than asking him to read it independently
b. Supplying him with an audio version of the textbook
c. Providing him with a printed outline of each chapter's main points
d. Giving him access to a multimedia version of the textbook to view on his computer

22. Mr. Davis notes that Alex, an ELL, often omits the *ed* ending on past tense verbs. How can Mr. Davis address this skill with Alex most effectively?

a. During a shared writing activity about a recent science experiment, Mr. Davis should call attention to the *-ed* endings of the verbs as they are written, explaining that they are needed because the activity happened in the past.
b. When Alex omits an *-ed* ending in a spoken word, Mr. Davis should correct the error immediately and help Alex restate the sentence correctly.
c. Mr. Davis should make words with *-ed* endings the focus of Alex's weekly spelling list.
d. Mr. Davis should ask Alex to find and underline all the words containing *-ed* endings in a printed article.

23. William, a third-grade student, recently wrote, "The cars drives down the street," in his writing journal. His teacher notices that he makes similar errors in other sentences he writes. He also makes these types of errors when reading. For example, he recently said, "The birds flies in the sky," while reading a text. Which grammatical skill should the teacher work on with William?

a. Pronoun-antecedent agreement
b. Consistent verb tenses
c. Subject-verb agreement
d. Complex sentences

24. A kindergarten teacher is administering a reading assessment to her students. She dictates some CVC words and asks students to write them down on paper. The words she dictates are *cat* and *cot*. One student writes the following responses on her paper.

bhp
wpi

Which skill should the teacher focus on first with this student?

a. Phonological awareness
b. Alphabetic principle
c. Phonics generalizations
d. Blending

25. A teacher uses a mixture of whole-group and small-group reading instruction. Which of the following activities would be the best choice for a whole-group lesson rather than small-group or individualized instruction?

a. Practice applying specific phonics skills
b. Independent reading of unfamiliar texts
c. Analyzing character development after the teacher reads a novel aloud
d. Spelling patterns

26. In which of the following sentences would it be most appropriate to suggest that a first-grade student use the "sound it out" strategy to decode the underlined word?

a. The child started to tear the wrapping paper off the gift.
b. The chain on the swing was squeaky.
c. The kitten was hiding behind the curtain.
d. The dolphin swam across the ocean.

27. Which of the following options best demonstrates a kinesthetic activity to build sight word recognition?

a. Circling sight words found in a magazine article
b. Building sight words with letter tiles
c. Reading books containing numerous sight words
d. Hopping along sight words written in chalk

28. Which theory suggests that there is no fixed meaning in any text, and that the meaning is determined by each individual's interactions with the text based on prior knowledge and experiences?

a. Louise Rosenblatt's transactional theory of the literary work
b. Howard Gardner's theory of multiple intelligences
c. David Perkins' theory of learnable intelligence
d. Lev Vygotsky's social development theory

29. The use of which graphic organizer best supports schema theory?

a. Problem-solution chart
b. Think-pair-share chart
c. Sequence chain
d. KWL chart

30. Which of the following teacher actions would most effectively encourage reading development in students' home environments?

a. Reminding students to read with their parents each day
b. Sending home a weekly update listing the phonics skills the class practiced
c. Sending home a list of weekly spelling words for students to memorize
d. Sending home leveled texts for students to read with family members

31. A second-grade teacher is planning a lesson on adjectives and will ask students to locate 10 adjectives in a text. Which modified activity would be the most appropriate way for the teacher to engage advanced students in exploring adjectives?

a. Asking them to locate 20 adjectives in the text
b. Asking students to locate vague adjectives in the text and then replace them with more specific adjectives
c. Pairing the proficient readers with struggling readers to complete the activity
d. Assigning the students an additional practice paper to complete after finding the 10 adjectives

32. While speaking to his friend, a fifth-grade student says, "Hey, you should read this book. It's awesome." Later, while presenting an oral book report in front of his class and teacher, he says, "This book is full of suspense. The author leaves you wondering if the main character will be rescued from the mountain before it is too late. I highly recommend you read it to find out if he is rescued in time." This example best demonstrates the role of what in language usage?

a. Social context
b. Cultural context
c. Contextual clues
d. Personal context

33. Which instructional strategy would be most appropriate to assist a student with retention difficulties in analyzing the plot of a fictional text?

a. Providing the student with a story map
b. Having the student read the story twice before responding to questions
c. Playing an audio version of the story rather than having the student read a printed version
d. Asking the student to complete a KWL chart before and after reading

34. Which of the following examples best demonstrates a child who has not yet developed an understanding of book concepts?

a. A first-grade student always looks to the pictures to figure out unknown words rather than using phonics strategies.
b. A preschool student often holds books upside down and turns pages randomly.
c. A kindergarten student inconsistently uses a return sweep and sometimes forgets where to go next after completing a line of text.
d. A first-grade student sometimes points to one printed word for every two or three spoken words.

35. Which of the following examples best describes a predictable text that is most appropriate for emergent readers to read independently?

a. A fantasy book containing a common theme, such as friendship, that students can relate to
b. A chapter book that is part of a popular series, whose characters students are familiar with
c. A fairy tale with a clear protagonist and antagonist, which helps students to predict the ending
d. A book in which every page states, "I see a ..." followed by a picture to complete the sentence

36. Which of the following words has the most phonemes?

a. Sheet
b. Hand
c. Right
d. Sea

37. Which of the following words has exactly three syllables?

a. House
b. Relentless
c. Beauty
d. Destructible

38. Which of the following words has exactly two morphemes?

a. Defrosting
b. Realigned
c. Dogs
d. Tip

39. A sentence in a book states, "They had several chores to do." Which of the following examples demonstrates a visual error, if stated by a student reading the text?

a. They had several jobs to do.
b. They had seven chores to do.
c. They had chores to do.
d. They had many chores to do.

40. A sentence in a book states, "The furry dog chases the stick." Which of the following examples demonstrates a structural error, if stated by a student reading the text?

a. The furry dog chases the branch.
b. The furry dog chases the big stick.
c. The fuzzy dog chases the stick.
d. The furry dog chased the stick.

41. A sentence in a book states, "It is fun to play checkers." Which of the following examples demonstrates an error related to meaning, if stated by a student reading the text?

a. It is fun playing checkers.
b. It is fun to play chess.
c. It is fun to play games.
d. It is fun to play checkers with friends.

42. A fourth-grade teacher asks her students an open-ended question about the author's purpose relating to a novel they are reading. She gives students a few minutes to think about their personal responses before discussing them with partners for a few additional minutes. Finally, she asks students to discuss their responses as a class. Which instructional strategy is the teacher using?

a. Think-pair-share
b. Jigsaw
c. Close reading
d. Cloze reading

43. A parent of a first-grade student is concerned about her child's use of phonetic spelling. She is concerned that her daughter is not spelling enough words conventionally and is developing habits that will be difficult to overcome. She presents the following sentence that her daughter recently wrote as an example:

A leprd haz spots.

What would be the most appropriate response to the parent?

a. Going forward, an adult should assist the child during writing tasks and confirm the spelling of each unknown word.
b. Students in this stage typically write the sounds that they hear, and this stage is a stepping stone to conventional spelling development.
c. At this age, the student should be using more conventional spelling, and a phonics intervention plan should be created.
d. The student should be encouraged to use a dictionary to confirm spellings of unknown words.

44. Which of the following options would be the most effective way to modify a cloze reading passage for struggling readers to assist them with completing the task while still allowing them to practice the skill?

a. Providing the first few letters of each answer
b. Including a word bank
c. Having students work in pairs
d. Including no more than three omitted words

45. Kindergarten students are viewing a digital storybook on the computer. As each word is read aloud, it is highlighted on the screen. Which two concepts of print does this highlighting best assist students with developing?

a. Directionality and one-to-one correspondence
b. Letter and word concepts
c. Book awareness and book handling skills
d. Word spacing and awareness of the relationship between the text and illustrations

46. Which of the following instructional strategies best demonstrates a way to prevent letter confusion in kindergarten students?

a. Introducing the letters in alphabetical order
b. Teaching visually similar letters, such as *b* and *d*, separately
c. Requiring students to master each letter before introducing the next letter
d. Focusing more on letter sounds than on letter names

47. Which of the following words consists of one free morpheme and one affix?

a. Unhelpful
b. Previewing
c. Truck
d. Friendless

48. Which of the following questions requires students to make an inference about a fictional text?

a. Did the author support her points with strong evidence?
b. How do you think the character felt when she said that?
c. What do you think will happen next?
d. Does this character remind you of any characters in other books you have read?

49. Which of the following options best demonstrates a kindergarten teacher differentiating phonics instruction for her diverse group of students?

a. Asking struggling readers to decode two CVC words and asking highly proficient readers to decode 10 CVC words
b. Asking struggling readers to decode CVC words and asking highly proficient readers to write CVC words in sentences
c. Asking struggling readers to decode CVC words and asking highly proficient readers to decode words with consonant blends
d. Having struggling and proficient readers work in pairs to decode CVC words

50. A kindergarten teacher notices that one of his students consistently understands and follows directions that are spoken to him. However, when he speaks in any situation, his sentences are often missing key words and don't make sense. The student is demonstrating difficulties with what?

a. Expressive language
b. Receptive language
c. Pragmatic language
d. Articulation

51. Which of the following examples best demonstrates an intensive intervention plan for a student whose assessment results show she is performing below benchmark levels in decoding consonant blends?

a. Sending home leveled readers containing numerous consonant blends for the student to read with family members
b. Requiring the student to complete independent activities related to consonant blends during the daily word work station
c. Adding 15 minutes of small-group instruction on consonant blends four times per week
d. Teaching a whole-class lesson on consonant blends, followed by multiple independent practice activities

52. A teacher is introducing a new phonics skill to her students. She begins with explicit instruction on the skill, followed by modeling. Which instructional component should come next?

a. Independent practice
b. Guided practice
c. Generalization
d. Feedback

53. A fifth-grade teacher introduces the skill of underlining text evidence to answer comprehension questions. He then models how to use this strategy using a sample text and related questions. Next, the class uses the strategy together to answer a new set of questions, with the teacher providing feedback on each attempt. Which activity would be the best choice to come next?

a. Give students a passage and questions to complete independently using the underlining strategy.
b. Reteach how to use the underlining strategy using different examples.
c. Ask students to use this strategy when they take tests in the future.
d. Test students on their ability to use the underlining strategy to answer comprehension questions.

54. Which example best demonstrates the writing or drawing of *candy* typical of a child in the transitional stage of writing development?

a. 
b. Csce
c. Cande
d. Candy

55. Which of the following options best demonstrates a specific and measurable reading intervention goal for a first grader?

a. The student will increase his score on the DIBELS Nonsense Word Fluency: Whole Words Read assessment from 10 to 15 by May 30 of this year.
b. The student will read at a DRA level 14.
c. The student will increase his oral reading rate on the DIBELS: Oral Reading Fluency assessment by December 15 of this year.
d. The student will meet grade-level benchmarks on the DRA.

56. What is orthographic processing?

a. The ability to separate spoken words into component sounds
b. Understanding the predictable sound each letter makes
c. Recognizing letter patterns that make up words or word parts
d. Understanding spoken words

57. Which of the following words contains a phonogram produced by three letters?

a. Tack
b. Hit
c. Bleak
d. Light

58. Cause and effect, compare and contrast, and time order are all examples of what?

a. Literary devices
b. Literary elements
c. Genres
d. Text structures

59. A second grader is reading a page from a narrative text. Halfway through the page, he stops and says, "Wait! This doesn't make sense. I think I read something wrong." What type of skill is the student demonstrating?

a. Decoding skills
b. Metacognitive skills
c. Evaluative skills
d. Application skills

60. A sixth-grade student is struggling to comprehend several different types of nonfiction texts. Which strategy would be most likely to assist him with this difficulty?

a. Asking him to reread the text multiple times to locate key information
b. Providing him with a story map to complete while reading
c. Teaching him to recognize the features of different nonfiction text structures
d. Asking him to summarize the main points of each text

61. A teacher introduces a new book about water conservation to students and says, "As you read this book, locate three ways you can conserve water at home." What is her primary reason for this statement?

a. To encourage students to consider the author's purpose
b. To help students set a purpose for reading
c. To activate students' prior knowledge
d. To encourage students to make text-to-text connections

62. Students in a fourth-grade class are reading and analyzing a fictional book about a girl, Samantha, who finds a wallet in the parking lot of a store. Which student response best demonstrates a prediction made using text evidence?

a. I think the book is mostly about honesty because Samantha ultimately decided to return the money she found.
b. I think Samantha will return the money because that is what I would do in her situation.
c. I think the author wrote the book to teach readers about the importance of being honest.
d. I think Samantha will decide to return the money because this chapter ends with her thinking about the bills the owner may need to pay with the money inside.

63. Third-grade students are reading a short story containing talking animals as the main characters. The story is clearly designed to teach readers a lesson. This story belongs to which genre of fiction?

a. Realistic fiction
b. Historical fiction
c. Fables
d. Mysteries

64. Joseph is reading a book with fictional characters who live in modern times but travel back to the American Revolution to fight with the colonial soldiers. This book contains elements of which two genres of fiction?

a. Folktales and realistic fiction
b. Fantasy and historical fiction
c. Fable and fantasy
d. Historical fiction and folktale

65. Elizabeth, a sixth-grade student, is researching Hellen Keller's life before writing a biographical report about her. The report will include information about both her childhood and adulthood, along with information about how she learned to communicate over time. When selecting books to use as sources and while writing her own report, which type of text structure would best fit her purposes?

a. Cause and effect
b. Time-order
c. Compare and contrast
d. Descriptive

66. A preschool teacher is reading nursery rhymes to students, putting deliberate emphasis on the rhyming words. Which reading-related skill is she trying to develop in her students?

a. Phonological awareness
b. Phonemic awareness
c. Alphabetic principle
d. Phonics

67. A first-grade teacher is teaching his students about different spelling patterns that can be used to produce short vowel sounds. Which of the following words should he use to demonstrate the use of the floss rule?

a. Match
b. Glass
c. Sip
d. Trap

68. A second-grade class is listening to a read-aloud of a fictional text about Thanksgiving Day in America. One student has recently moved to America and is unfamiliar with the holiday. Which of the following options is the most effective way for the teacher to address this issue with the student?

a. Ask the student to retell the story after listening to it to assess comprehension.
b. Provide background information on Thanksgiving before reading, relating it to traditions the student is familiar with.
c. Provide the student with a written outline of the key elements in the story before reading.
d. After reading, describe the key features of the story and holiday again with different language than what was used in the book.

69. Which of the following statements is typically true of literature circles?

a. All students within a classroom read and discuss the same book.
b. Teachers predetermine the questions and concepts that will be discussed.
c. Students have choices about the books they read.
d. Groups remain static throughout the year.

70. A teacher wants to introduce the concept of connotative and denotative meanings while reading a novel. He plans to use character traits as a way to introduce this topic. Which set of words to describe a character would best help him introduce and explain connotative and denotative word meanings?

a. Kind and nice
b. Happy and joyful
c. Determined and persistent
d. Frugal and cheap

71. Which literary term describes the use of repeated vowel sounds in nearby words, such as in the sentence, "The splotchy drops dotted the window"?

a. Onomatopoeia
b. Alliteration
c. Consonance
d. Assonance

72. Which term describes an unstressed central vowel sound, such as the sound made by the *a* in *around*?

a. Digraph
b. Long
c. Diphthong
d. Schwa

73. A second-grade teacher is reading a student's journal entry and sees the following set of sentences:

"I lisened to a great story. Then my teacher asked a question, and I ansered it."

Based on these sentences, which skill would be most beneficial for the teacher to focus on with the student?

a. Consonant blends
b. Consonant digraphs
c. Silent letter spelling patterns
d. Subject/verb agreement

74. A first-grade student struggles to decode words containing *oo* in their spellings because that vowel combination makes two common sounds. Which prompt would be most likely to assist the student with decoding these words when encountered in texts?

a. Look for parts of the word you already know.
b. Use visual clues to guess the word and make sure that your guess looks right.
c. Read the word both ways in the sentence to see which way makes sense.
d. Think of similar words you know that have the same spelling pattern.

Refer to the following for question 75:

A fourth-grade student struggles to decode several words in her science textbook, including *organism*, *conclusion*, and *prediction*.

75. Which text feature could the teacher direct the student to use to best assist with this difficulty?

a. Table of contents
b. Headings
c. Index
d. Glossary

76. What does the term *story grammar* refer to?

a. The general structure of a story, including story elements
b. The ability to use conventions of English correctly when composing fictional stories
c. The ability to apply rules of syntax to decode unknown words in stories
d. The main idea of a story

77. Which set of terms demonstrates a synonym pair?

a. *Selfish* and *generous*
b. *Conceited* and *pompous*
c. *Photograph* and *photosynthesis*
d. *Steel* and *steal*

78. Which set of words demonstrates an antonym pair?

a. *Build* and *construct*
b. *Peer* (to look at) and *peer* (someone of similar age or status)
c. *Shake* and *cake*
d. *Drowsy* and *alert*

79. Students in a fifth-grade class are breaking the word *invisible* into its component parts. They identify the prefix *in-*, the root *vis*, and the suffix *-ible*, along with the meanings of each part. What type of activity is being demonstrated?

a. Miscue analysis
b. Structural analysis
c. Syllabification
d. Decoding

80. Which of the following options is true of children in the pre-alphabetic stage of word learning?

a. Children do not use any letter/sound relationships to decode words.
b. Children use letter/sound relationships to correctly decode the initial or final sounds in words.
c. Children use letter/sound relationships to correctly decode all sounds in simple, age-appropriate words.
d. Children recognize and use letter groupings, along with letter/sound relationships, to decode words.

81. Character maps, fact and opinion charts, 5Ws charts, and webs are all examples of what?

a. Literary elements
b. Genres
c. Text features
d. Graphic organizers

82. Which of the following sentences would best help model the concept of figurative language?

a. The sky was dark and gray, warning that a storm was approaching.
b. The snow was a wet blanket covering the earth.
c. Taking care of a puppy requires time and patience.
d. The cold, wet raindrops splashed on my glasses and made it difficult to see.

83. The study of historical origins of words is known as what?

a. Morphology
b. Linguistics
c. Semantics
d. Etymology

84. Which of the following options best describes decodable texts?

a. They contain a predictable text structure that allows emergent readers to guess what will come next.
b. They allow students to apply newly learned phonics skills while reading new texts.
c. They contain a large amount of content-related words to reinforce vocabulary development.
d. They are books with complex plot development that are ideal for close reading analysis.

85. Which of the following spelling patterns is usually taught to children first?

a. CVCe
b. CVVC
c. CVC
d. CCVC

86. Which of the following statements is true regarding screening and diagnostic assessments?

a. Screening assessments provide more thorough information than diagnostic assessments about students' specific strengths and needs.
b. Screening assessments are typically used to confirm diagnostic assessment results.
c. Screening assessments are used to identify students who may be at future risk of academic difficulties and may benefit from interventions.
d. Diagnostic assessments are used to identify students who may be at future risk of academic difficulties and may benefit from interventions.

87. The use of analogies is most appropriate for helping students achieve which instructional objective?

a. Analyzing common roots and affixes
b. Defining words
c. Identifying word origins
d. Recognizing the relationships between words

88. A kindergarten teacher says the words *tap* and *top* aloud. She asks students to identify whether the sound that is different is found in the beginning, middle, or ending of the words. Which skill does this activity practice?

a. Phoneme substitution
b. Phoneme discrimination
c. Phoneme deletion
d. Phoneme insertion

89. Olivia, a first-grade student, has a reading intervention plan to improve her decoding of CVCe words. In addition to working with the teacher in a small group each day, Olivia's teacher gives her 10 new CVCe words to decode each Friday. The number of words read correctly is recorded on a graph, and the teacher notes any improvement made from the previous weeks. Which type of assessment is the teacher demonstrating?

a. Progress monitoring
b. Screening assessment
c. Summative assessment
d. Norm-referenced assessment

90. Students in a second-grade classroom are exploring and building words that contain *eigh*. Which layer of orthography are they exploring?

a. Alphabet layer
b. Pattern layer
c. Meaning layer
d. Conventional layer

91. Which of the following statements is true regarding word walls?

a. They should mainly focus on content-related words.
b. They should contain only words that are difficult for students to spell independently.
c. They should be flexible, allowing words to be added and removed throughout the year.
d. They are only needed for students in the emergent stage of reading development.

92. Prekindergarten students tell their teacher, Mr. Clark, that they want to write about their field trip to the zoo. Mr. Clark writes down the students' sentences on chart paper, and then reads them back to the class, pointing to each word and modeling appropriate fluency. After reading the story multiple times, Mr. Clark invites the students to read with him. Which type of interaction is Mr. Clark demonstrating?

a. Language experience approach
b. Writing workshop
c. Trait-based writing
d. Modeled writing

93. Reciprocal teaching activities focus on four main reading strategies. What is the fourth strategy, in addition to summarizing, questioning, and predicting?

a. Evaluating
b. Connecting
c. Retelling
d. Clarifying

94. Which of the following questions is focused on students' aesthetic responses to a text?

a. Which character is the protagonist in the story?
b. What is the conflict in the story?
c. How did you feel when the character was being treated poorly by her friends?
d. What genre does this story fit into?

95. Before reading a nonfiction book about habitats, students are given a list of statements about the content and asked if they agree or disagree with them. After reading, they return to the list and their initial responses and indicate if they still agree with their choices or if their thoughts have changed as a result of new information gained while reading. What type of tool does this example describe?

a. Storyboard
b. Anticipation guide
c. Concept map
d. Outline

96. A fifth-grade teacher is helping his students analyze how varied sentence structure contributes to the tone and mood of a text. Which of the following sentences should he use if he wants to model a complex sentence?

a. Michael ate pancakes for breakfast.
b. Michael ate breakfast and brushed his teeth.
c. Before going to school, Michael brushed his teeth.
d. Michael ate breakfast, and he brushed his teeth.

97. A teacher wants his students to become familiar with a wide range of genres and text structures. Which of the following options would best help him achieve this goal?

a. Displaying posters describing different genres and text structures in the classroom
b. Rewarding students who choose to read a variety of different types of books during independent reading time
c. Selecting books from different genres and with different text structures for read-alouds and shared reading activities
d. Sending home a list of varied books and encouraging students to check them out from their local libraries

98. Which of the following sentences contains a compound word?

a. The children played soccer in the backyard.
b. All of the children had fun at the picnic in the park.
c. Many families cheered for their favorite teams during the soccer game.
d. The players were tired and thirsty after they finished the soccer game.

99. In which of the following examples does the root word change when the suffix *-ment* is added?

a. Treat
b. Replace
c. Establish
d. Argue

100. Which of the following best describes Chomsky's theory of Universal Grammar?

a. All languages have a level of structure in common.
b. All languages have a similar order of acquisition.
c. All languages can be acquired in the same amount of time.
d. All languages have equivalent rules, though ordering may be different.

Constructed Response

1. Caleb is a first-grade student who is writing in his journal. The topic of his entry is his recent field trip to the apple orchard. Caleb's entry is shown below.

My clas went to the apple orchrd yestrday. We tastd apple cidr and ate donuts. We also got to go on a hayride. We lernd about how sum apples are sweet and sum apples are sowr. We walkd arownd and lookd at differnt apple trees. It was fun.

Using knowledge of writing development (e.g., understanding of concepts of print, understanding of alphabetic principle, knowledge of high-frequency words, phonics skills), write a response in which you both:

- Identify some of Caleb's strengths related to writing words and sentences.
- Identify some of Caleb's weaknesses related to writing words and sentences.

Use evidence from Caleb's response to support your answer.

2. Alicia is in her first month of kindergarten. Her teacher gives her a book containing the following pages.

Cover: *The Park* by John Smith

Page 1: It is fun to swing. (picture of a swing)

Page 2: It is fun to slide. (picture of a slide)

Page 3: It is fun to run. (picture of kids running)

Page 4: It is fun to climb. (picture of a jungle gym)

Page 5: The park is fun.

The teacher provides Alicia with a series of prompts and records her responses. The prompts and responses are shown in the table below.

Teacher's Prompts	Alicia's Responses
Show me how to hold the book.	Holds the book right-side up
Show me the front of the book.	Points to the front of the book
Show me the back of the book.	Points to the back of the book
Show me the title of the book.	Points to *The Park* on the front cover
Show me where to start reading the book.	Opens the book and points to page 3

(on page 3) Show me where to begin reading on this page.	Points to the word "fun"
Show me with your finger which way I go as I read this page.	Moves her finger back and forth across the page in a zigzag fashion several times quickly
(on page 3) Point to the words as I read them.	Points to "It" three times in a row, then quickly moves her finger across the rest of the text.

Using knowledge of concepts of print, write a response in which you both:

- Identify some of Alicia's strengths relating to concepts of print.
- Identify some of Alicia's weaknesses relating to concepts of print.

Use evidence from the teacher's observations of Alicia to support your answer.

Answer Key and Explanations for Test #2

Multiple Choice Questions

1. B: Personification refers to giving humanlike qualities to nonhuman objects. This is demonstrated when Isabella describes the river as *dancing*, which is a human action. A simile is a comparison between two things using the word *like* or *as*. Onomatopoeia refers to sound words, and hyperbole is an exaggeration used for emphasis.

2. C: Allusion is a literary device where references are made to commonly known people or events without describing them explicitly. In this example, readers are expected to understand that the reference to Dr. Jekyll and Mr. Hyde means that the employee never knows whether his boss will be pleasant or difficult each day. Foreshadowing refers to clues in the text that hint at future events. Irony is used to signify that something is the opposite of what is expected. Puns are a type of humorous wordplay involving words that have multiple meanings.

3. B: Caleb is stating that nobody likes meatloaf after observing that a small sample of the school population does not appear to like it. He is drawing conclusions based on insufficient data, which is an overgeneralization. An illogical conclusion occurs when someone draws conclusions about the relationships between two things without data supporting the relationship. Personal bias occurs when conclusions are based on personal opinions rather than data. Circular reasoning occurs when someone supports a claim by restating the same claim rather than by providing new data.

4. D: When students take away a sound in a word and say what new word they are left with, they are practicing phoneme deletion. Onset and rime manipulation involve breaking or combining a word between the first sound and the remainder of the word. Segmenting involves breaking a word into its individual sounds. Phoneme isolation involves identifying a specific phoneme within a word.

5. C: When students match picture cards with the consonant blends they begin with, they are using their understanding of the relationships between letters and the sounds they make. Therefore, it is a phonics activity. Choice A is a phonological awareness activity because it deals with sounds rather than letter/sound relationships. Choice B is a letter identification activity because students are matching letters to their names without addressing the sounds they make. Choice D is a comprehension activity because students are listening to a story and identifying story elements. They are not decoding the text independently.

6. D: The word *maple* begins with an open syllable, spelled *ma*. Open syllables end with a vowel and usually have a long vowel sound. Knowing this will help the student decode this word and other words with open syllables. This word does not contain any vowel digraph pairs, r-controlled vowels, or closed syllables. Vowel digraph pairs consist of two vowels that together make one sound. R-controlled vowels consist of a vowel before the letter *r*. Closed syllables end with a consonant and usually have a short vowel sound.

7. A: While all of these options are important and beneficial for reading development, research has indicated that phonemic awareness is one of the strongest predictors of early reading success. Understanding that words are made up of individual sounds assists with learning the letter/sound relationships in phonics. These relationships are used to decode words.

8. B: The word *manuscript* has the Latin root *manu*, meaning *hand*, and the Latin root *script*, meaning *write*. By recognizing these roots, a reader can determine that the word *manuscript* means something written by hand. *Trees* does not contain any Greek or Latin roots that could be identified to determine the word meaning. *Butterfly* is a compound word, but the *butter* component does not assist with the meaning of the compound word. Although *ceiling* has the inflectional ending *-ing*, it is unlikely to assist students with identifying the meaning of the word when added to *ceil*.

9. D: All of the listed options can assist students with developing reading skills, and students will have individual opinions regarding preferred activities. However, reading is a social experience that helps children learn about themselves and the world around them. Using language creatively, such as through rhyming, helps them understand all of the ways that language can be used. Reading and discussing stories together is also a social experience that connects readers and makes them part of a community of learners. These benefits will likely contribute to a love of reading more than practicing isolated skills.

10. B: Academic vocabulary refers to words typically used in school conversations and texts. They are words related to the processes and concepts taught in multiple subject areas. Listening vocabulary refers to words that a person can understand when heard aloud. Children can often understand words that they hear before using them in their own speech and writing. Receptive vocabulary refers to all of the words that a person can understand when encountered in speech or writing. Expressive vocabulary refers to all of the words that a person can correctly use in his or her own speech or writing.

11. C: The words in this set can be grouped into two categories: academic vocabulary and content vocabulary. Academic vocabulary words are commonly used in school but are not specific to one subject area. For example, students may compare shapes in math, compare living things in science, and compare characters in reading. Content vocabulary refers to words related to one specific subject area. *Organism*, *cell*, and *habitat* are typically used in science.

12. B: In reader's theater, students are given roles in an informal play and practice their lines repeatedly before performing for the class. As students practice reading their lines repeatedly, they build reading fluency. Students typically read from their scripts during reader's theater, so memorization is not required. Additionally, students usually do not use any costumes or props, and they typically use existing scripts rather than writing their own.

13. D: Although all of the skills listed are part of digital literacy, the main focus of this assignment is to create writing on the same topic for two very different audiences. Students will therefore need to know how to adjust the formality of their writing so that it is appropriate for each audience. A post on the school website, which will be seen by numerous community members, should use a more formal tone than an email to a friend. Therefore, choice D is the most relevant skill for this particular assignment.

14. C: Prekindergarten students are likely in the emergent stage of reading development, where they are developing an understanding of the concepts of print. In this stage, they are in the beginning stages of learning to recognize letters and letter/sound relationships. Therefore, an activity that focuses on letter identification is most developmentally appropriate. The other activities require more complex phonics skills and would be more appropriate for students in the early stage of reading development.

15. B: This graphic organizer could be used to help the student identify the main elements of the story, including the characters, problem, plot, and resolution. Therefore, it could be used to help the student summarize the story. It does not contain any prompts requiring the student to use the higher-level thinking skills required to infer, draw conclusions, or evaluate.

16. D: To allow Joshua more time and energy to focus on his essay, he can record only key words and phrases in his notes rather than writing complete sentences. This will also make it easier for him to locate the key information in his notes when he is ready to add it to his essay. Grouping notes into categories and using visuals can be beneficial, but based on Joshua's notes, recording the key words and phrases is the most pressing need. Recording only a few facts may not provide enough information to complete an entire three-paragraph essay, so it would be more helpful to record additional facts in a more concise manner.

17. C: The teacher is demonstrating a think-aloud, or sharing her thinking process as she uses a reading strategy. In this example, she explains her thoughts as she uses context clues to determine the meaning of an unknown word. Mental images and visualizations both refer to the pictures that readers get in their minds when they read. Predictions are logical guesses about what might happen in a text.

18. B: Closed syllables end with consonants and show readers places where words can be divided during decoding. By dividing the words into syllables, Laura can sound out *rab-bit* and *prob-lem* more easily. Open syllables end with vowels, and these words do not contain open syllables. If Laura divides the words into sections with CVCC spelling patterns, she will not be dividing them into syllables, which will make decoding more difficult. Double consonants occur when the same consonant appears twice in a row in a word. Although *rabbit* has a double consonant (the two *b's*), *problem* does not.

19. A: An inflectional ending is a letter or group of letters added to the end of a root word. It is sometimes used to change the tense of the root word, as in the case of adding *ed* to *jump* to indicate past tense. Both *-ed* and *-ing* are inflectional endings. The words in choice B end in diphthongs, which are formed when two vowel sounds are combined within a syllable. The words in choice C end in consonant digraphs, or two or more consonants that are combined to form a new sound. The words in choice D rhyme, and they use different spelling patterns to make the same sound.

20. C: In choice C, students listen and watch as their teacher reads a print-based book aloud, and then they use a digital tool to create a multimedia presentation. This combines both digital and print-based media. Choice A consists of two print-based activities. Choices B and D each contain two digital activities.

21. D: If the student is having difficulties with comprehension rather than decoding, he will likely benefit from having the information represented in multiple ways. Seeing visual representations of the words and content may assist him with comprehension. Additionally, multimedia textbooks often contain features like hyperlinked vocabulary words that display definitions when clicked. Choices A and B would only read the same vocabulary words aloud without any additional explanation or visuals to assist with comprehension. An outline also presents the information in text rather than focusing on visual clues.

22. A: Grammatical skills can be learned more effectively when they are taught and practiced in context. In choice A, Mr. Davis is calling attention to the skill during an authentic writing task. Correcting an ELL's grammatical errors repeatedly in spoken conversations can negatively affect the student's confidence. While adding *-ed* words to the spelling list and identifying them in an article can assist with learning the skill, these activities do not allow the student to practice using the skill in context as part of an authentic activity.

23. C: William is making errors in subject-verb agreement. Singular nouns should be paired with singular verbs, and plural nouns should be paired with plural verbs. Pronoun-antecedent agreement refers to ensuring that pronouns agree with their antecedents in number and gender. The sentences in this example do not include pronouns. There are no errors present in verb tense or sentence complexity. Verb consistency refers to ensuring that the verbs within a piece of writing use the same tense. Complex sentences are sentences that contain at least one dependent and independent clause.

24. B: The student's responses include random strings of letters that do not correlate with the sounds in the spoken words. Additionally, she has represented the /c/ sound at the beginning of each word differently in her responses. Understanding that letters make predictable sounds is part of the alphabetic principle. Her three-letter responses indicate that she has some phonological awareness skills. She knows there are three sounds in each word, but she is not aware of which letters are used to represent each sound. Teaching phonics generalizations will be more helpful after the student has developed an awareness of the alphabetic principle and consistently matches letters to their sounds.

25. C: One of the challenges of large-group instruction is meeting the needs of diverse learners. Reading a novel aloud helps to make the content accessible to all learners. If students were to read it independently, as in choice B, the text would likely not be challenging enough for some readers and too difficult for others. Therefore, basing a comprehension lesson on a book that was read aloud assists all students with participating. While teachers sometimes introduce and practice phonics skills in large groups, students are likely to have differing skill levels in this area. Proficient first-grade readers, for example, may read consonant blends and digraphs with ease, which struggling readers may still be learning the alphabetic principle. Students in a classroom are also likely to have vastly different spelling skills, making the need for differentiation important.

26. B: The word *chain* contains a common consonant digraph, *ch*; and two vowels together, *ai*, which make the /ā/ sound. Recognizing these patterns will make the word easy to sound out. In choice A, the two vowels in *tear* do not make the /ē/ sound, as would likely be expected. The sound produced by *ain* in *curtain* makes it more difficult for a first grader to sound out, as does the sound of the *c* in *ocean*.

27. D: When students participate in kinesthetic activities, they are physically engaged in the learning process. These activities involve movement, such as hopping along the sight words written in chalk. While the other activities can also be used to practice sight words and may involve tactile experiences, they involve less movement and physical activity than hopping.

28. A: Louise Rosenblatt's transactional theory of the literary work suggests that reading is a transaction between the reader and the text, and different readers may take different meaning from the same text. Vygotsky's social development theory suggests that children interact in various social and cultural contexts through which cognitive development takes place. David Perkins theorized that humans have three types of intelligence: neural, experiential, and reflective. While neural intelligence is determined by genetics, experiential and reflective intelligence can be developed over time and should be fostered through learning experiences. According to Gardner's theory, there are eight different types of intelligences, and each type has different strengths and learning preferences.

29. D: Schema theory suggests that when people encounter new concepts, the newly learned knowledge gets organized into units called schemata. When they encounter related information in the future, they access their existing schemata to make sense of it. Therefore, a KWL chart, which helps students relate a topic to existing knowledge, best supports schema theory. The remaining types of graphic organizers support reading development but do not specifically require students to activate prior knowledge.

30. D: Sending home leveled texts ensures that families have access to books in students' instructional reading levels. Providing the books allows students to read immediately and free of charge without requiring any trips to a library or bookstore. Choice A is also helpful, but without providing appropriate books, there is no guarantee that students will have access to reading materials. Notifying parents of which phonics skills the class practiced can also be helpful, but without providing additional information or materials, parents may not know how to best help their children practice these skills. Studying spelling words addresses the words in isolation rather than providing opportunities to read in context and practice decoding, comprehension, and fluency.

31. B: Advanced readers and writers should be given opportunities to explore concepts using high-level thinking skills. If they have already mastered identifying adjectives, then evaluating adjective choices in a text and selecting stronger options would be a more challenging activity. Proficient readers and writers should not simply be given additional amounts of unchallenging work, as suggested in options A and D. Pairing students with differing skill levels can have instructional benefits, but the activities should be structured to ensure that both students benefit from the interactions.

32. A: The student is adjusting his language according to his current social situation. When speaking to a friend, he uses informal language. When presenting a report in front of the class and teacher, he switches to more formal language. Cultural context refers to the ways that messages are delivered and received based on differing cultural backgrounds and norms. Contextual clues are clues in a text that assist readers with determining the meanings of unknown words. Personal context refers to how communication is affected by an individual's age, gender, educational background, and other personal factors.

33. A: A story map outlines the main elements of the story, including the characters, setting, conflict, plot, and resolution. Recording these elements will assist the student in remembering and analyzing the story after it has been read. If the student has retention issues, he or she may not recall the story elements even after reading the story twice or listening to an audio version. A KWL chart can be used to activate prior knowledge and help the student reflect on what was learned, but it does not outline the story elements needed to analyze plot.

34. B: Book concepts refers to knowing how to hold and manipulate books. The preschool student in choice B is holding the book upside down and not turning pages from front to back, indicating she has not yet developed an understanding of book concepts. Choice A demonstrates a student who is relying on the semantic cueing system rather than using a variety of decoding strategies. Choice C demonstrates a student who has not yet mastered return sweep, and choice D demonstrates a student who has not yet mastered one-to-one correspondence.

35. D: Emergent readers are beginning to understand concepts of print and read very simple texts independently. Using short, repetitive sentences with picture support allows students to read these texts independently and practice concepts of print, such as one-to-one correspondence and understanding that the print carries the meaning. The other options contain predictable structures or characters that could assist emergent readers with comprehension if the texts are read aloud, but they would be too complex for students to decode independently.

36. B: Phonemes are the smallest units of sound in words. *Hand* has four phonemes: /h/, /ă/, /n/, and /d/. Choice A has three phonemes: /sh/, /ē/, and /t/. Choice C also has three phonemes: /r/, /ī/, and /t/. Choice D has two phonemes: /s/ and /ē/.

37. B: A syllable is a unit of pronunciation with one uninterrupted sound. Students can be taught to clap or tap to determine the number of syllables in a word. *Relentless* has three syllables: *re-lent-less*. Choice A has one syllable, choice C has two syllables, and choice D has four syllables.

38. C: A morpheme is the smallest unit of language with meaning, and a morpheme cannot be broken down any further without losing that meaning. *Dogs* has two morphemes: *dog* and the *s*, which indicates that the word is plural. Choice A has three morphemes: *de*, *frost*, and *ing*. Choice B also has three morphemes: *re*, *align*, and *ed*. Choice D has one morpheme: *tip*.

39. B: In choice B, the student substituted the word seven for several, and read the rest of the sentence correctly. The words seven and several are visually similar, as the first four letters are the same in each. Choices A and D demonstrate errors related to meaning, as the student substituted words that made sense in the sentences but were not visually similar to the existing words. Choice C contains an omission, as the student did not say several.

40. D: In choice D, the student read the sentence correctly, except for changing *chases* to *chased*. *Chased* still sounds right in the sentence, indicating that the student was using structural, or syntactic, cues to decode the word. In choice A, the student replaced *stick* with *branch*. *Branch* makes sense in the sentence, and it is not visually similar to the existing word. Choice B demonstrates an insertion, as the student added the word *big*. Choice C demonstrates a visual error, as the student replaced *furry* with *fuzzy*. Both words are visually similar.

41. C: In choice C, the student selected a word that makes sense in the sentence but does not share any visual similarities with the existing word. He was relying on meaning to decode the word. Choice A demonstrates a structural error, as the student changed the verb ending. However, the sentence he read still sounds right. Choice B demonstrates a visual error, as he substituted a word that is visually similar to the existing word. Choice D demonstrates an insertion, as he added a prepositional phrase to the end of the sentence.

42. A: This example describes the think-pair-share strategy, where a teacher poses a question, gives students time to think about their responses independently, and then puts them in pairs to discuss their responses together. Next, students discuss the responses as a whole class. In the jigsaw approach, students are put into small groups, and each student is assigned one portion of the content that he or she is responsible for learning and presenting to the group. Close reading involves multiple readings of the same text, exploring deeper layers each time. Cloze reading involves giving students a brief passage with some omitted words, which students fill in using clues or background knowledge.

43. B: Phonetic spelling is common at this age, as children write the sounds that they hear. They typically know how to spell a limited number of words conventionally. This is a typical stage of development, and over time, they will begin to spell more words conventionally as more phonics rules and spelling patterns are learned. Asking an adult or using a dictionary to confirm the spellings of all unknown words can slow down and inhibit the writing process. Additionally, as phonetic spelling is typical at this age and the student has spelled some words correctly, it is unlikely that an intervention is needed based solely on this information.

44. B: Including a word bank assists struggling readers with completing the activity by providing them with options to choose from. It is a way of scaffolding the activity while still requiring students to use context clues to determine which word is the best fit in each sentence. Providing the first few letters of each answer offers a bigger hint and may allow the student to guess the word easily. Cloze reading activities can be done in pairs, but it is possible that one student may supply the answer for the struggling reader. It is also possible for struggling readers to complete more than three questions with appropriate scaffolding.

45. A: By highlighting each word as it is read, children begin to understand that reading goes from left to right, which is known as directionality. They also begin to understand that each spoken word corresponds with one printed word, which is known as one-to-one correspondence. Letter and word concepts refer to an understanding that words are made up of individual letters. Book awareness and book handling skills include knowing how to hold a book and turn the pages correctly. Word spacing is the understanding that you include spaces between words on the page. The relationship between text and illustrations refers to an understanding that pictures provide clues about the meaning of the story.

46. B: Children tend to confuse letters that are visually similar, such as *b* and *d*. Introducing them separately helps to prevent confusion between them. While there are differing theories on which order to use when introducing letters, generally alphabetical order is not the most effective. Letters are sometimes grouped for instruction by the difficulty of their sounds, their formation, or relevance to the students (such as introducing letters in their names first). Letters may be introduced in small groups to allow students to practice them in context, and both letter sounds and letter names are important for students to learn.

47. D: A free morpheme, also known as a base word, can stand alone as a word. In choice D, *friend* is a free morpheme. An affix can be either a prefix or a suffix, and *friendless* has one suffix, *-less*. Choice A has a prefix, *un*; a free morpheme, *help*; and a suffix, *-ful*. Choice B has a prefix, *pre-*; a free morpheme, *view*; and a suffix, *-ing*. *Truck* only has a free morpheme and no affixes.

48. B: Inferring requires readers to use clues rather than explicit evidence to determine the author's meaning. Choice B requires students to use the character's statements to infer how he or she felt at the time. Choice A requires students to evaluate the writing. Choice C requires students to make a prediction. Choice D requires students to make a text-to-text connection.

49. C: Differentiation involves instructing students according to their individual strengths and needs as indicated by assessment data. Instruction should challenge students in their zones of proximal development to ensure that they learn new skills without becoming bored or frustrated. Choice C provides both groups of students with words at their appropriate levels of difficulty. Choice A involves simply giving extra words to highly proficient readers. If they have already mastered decoding CVC words, decoding many of them is likely to be boring and unchallenging. Similarly, if highly proficient readers have already mastered CVC words, writing them in sentences is likely to be less challenging or beneficial than learning to decode more complex words. While paired experiences can be beneficial in many situations, choice D does not provide more challenging words for the highly proficient readers, nor does it ensure that they will scaffold the struggling readers rather than decoding the words for them.

50. A: The student is demonstrating difficulties with expressive language, or ability to use spoken language to communicate as expected. Because he appears to understand and respond appropriately to speech he has heard, he is not displaying any difficulties with receptive language. Pragmatic language involves using language in ways that are appropriate for specific social situations. Because the student's difficulties are occurring in all contexts, they appear to be more related to expressive language than pragmatics. Articulation refers to difficulties making certain sounds. For example, sounds may be added or omitted from individual words. However, the student in this example is omitting entire words.

51. C: Choice C best demonstrates an intensive intervention plan because it includes small-group, targeted instruction at frequent, regularly scheduled times. The remaining options can assist the student with learning consonant blends, but they do not include frequent, regularly scheduled teacher interactions. During these intervention times, the teacher can provide instruction, supervise practice opportunities, offer feedback, monitor progress, and more.

52. B: Typically, guided practice follows modeling. Independent practice and application would then follow the guided practice, and generalization would come last. Feedback should be provided throughout multiple levels of instruction, particularly during the practice phases.

53. A: Generally, the sequence of instruction is as follows: explicit instruction, modeling, guided practice, independent practice and application, and generalization. The teacher has already completed the explicit instruction, modeling, and guided practice portion of the sequence. Therefore, independent practice and application would come next. Choice A best demonstrates this stage of instruction. Reteaching is only necessary if informal or formal assessments indicate that students did not learn the skill after the first attempt at instruction, which is not indicated in this example. Choice C represents the generalization stage, which typically comes after students have had independent practice with the skill. A formal assessment, such as a test, should also come after independent practice opportunities.

54. C: In the transitional stage of writing development, children begin to use capital and lowercase letters appropriately. They know how to spell many high-frequency words correctly and use knowledge of sound-symbol relationships to record the sounds they hear in more complex words. In choice C, the student has spelled the word almost correctly, using the *e* to represent the /ē/ formed by a *y* in the actual spelling of the word. Choice A demonstrates the preliterate stage of writing, where children use scribbles that are intended as writing. Choice B represents the emergent stage of writing, when children begin to form letters correctly. In this stage, they often write in all capital letters. At first, random strings of letters are used. Later, some sounds, such as the first and last sounds, may be represented correctly. Choice D demonstrates the fluent stage of writing development, where most words are spelled conventionally.

55. A: Choice A includes the current student performance level, the desired student performance level, the assessment used to determine the performance level, and the date the goal is expected to be achieved. Choice B only indicates the desired performance level and the assessment that will be used. Choice C indicates the assessment that will be used and the date the goal is expected to be achieved, but saying that it "will increase his oral reading rate" is too vague. It does not list the current or desired performance levels. Choice D only indicates the expected performance level and the assessment that will be used. It does not indicate the current performance level or the date the goal is expected to be achieved.

56. C: Orthographic processing refers to recognizing letter patterns that make up words or word parts. For example, a student may see the word *sight* and immediately recognize the *ight* pattern. The ability to separate spoken words into component sounds is a part of phonological awareness. Alphabetic principle is the understanding that each letter makes a predictable sound. Receptive language involves understanding spoken words.

57. D: A phonogram is a letter or group of letters that represent a single sound. In the word *light*, the letters *igh* together produce one sound, /ī/. The longest phonogram in choice A contains two letters, *ck*. Choice B contains only one-letter phonograms. The longest phonogram in choice C contains two letters, *ea*, which together produce the /ē/ sound.

58. D: Text structure refers to how a text is organized. Different text structures are used depending on the purpose for writing, and cause/effect, compare/contrast, and time-order text structures are all commonly used in nonfiction texts. Literary devices are techniques authors use in their writing to set a certain mood, emphasize a point, convey a description, or more. Literary elements refer to parts of texts, such as characters, setting, plot, conflict, and resolution. Genres refer to specific categories of texts, such as fantasies.

59. B: The student is monitoring his own reading and recognizing when something doesn't make sense. When he realizes that something doesn't make sense, he knows he has likely made an error. Monitoring one's own reading is a metacognitive skill. Decoding refers to the process of translating printed words into spoken words. Evaluative skills refer to the ability to evaluate something using evidence and/or prior knowledge. Application skills refer to the ability to apply skills in different contexts.

60. C: Understanding text features can help students locate key information in nonfiction texts. Additionally, understanding how different types of nonfiction texts are typically organized provides predictability and structure when reading new texts, which can assist with comprehension. While rereading and summarizing can be effective, asking the student to locate key information without any additional guidance or scaffolding is less likely to be effective. Story maps, which help students identify story elements, are used to assist with comprehending fictional texts.

61. B: By assigning students a task that will require them to focus on key pieces of information in the text, the teacher is helping students set a purpose for reading. She is not asking the students why the author wrote the book, which would encourage them to consider the author's purpose. Choice C is incorrect because she did not ask students what they already know about the topic of water conservation. Choice D is incorrect because she did not ask students to compare or contrast this text with any other texts they have read.

62. D: Choice D includes a prediction because the student tells what she thinks is going to happen in the story. She also includes text evidence by explaining how the clue at the end of the chapter influenced her prediction. Choice A shows the student describing the theme of the story. Choice B includes a prediction, but the student has supported it with a personal connection rather than using text evidence. Choice C shows the student's explanation of the author's purpose for writing the story.

63. C: Fables are a genre of fiction typically consisting of short stories centered around animals with humanlike traits. They usually include a lesson. Realistic fiction is a type of story that is made up but could really happen, so talking animals would not be included in this genre. Historical fiction is set during a specific period in history. Mysteries contain some type of crime or puzzle that must be solved.

64. B: This book contains elements of fantasy due to the time travel, and it contains elements of historical fiction with the characters' participation in the American Revolution. Choice A is incorrect because it is not a story passed down over time, so it is not a folktale. Additionally, while some portions of the story may seem realistic, the time traveling element makes it more fantasy than realistic fiction. Choice C is incorrect because the story doesn't focus on a moral or contain talking animals. Choice D is incorrect because it is not a folktale.

65. B: Because Elizabeth will be including facts about all stages of Helen Keller's life, as well as how she learned to communicate over time, a time-order, or chronological, text structure is the best fit. Time-order text structures tell the key points about the topic in sequential order. The other options could be used to share information about her life, but they would not be as logical of a fit for this type of biographical report, as they may weave back and forth between different time periods to show relationships between events.

66. A: Rhyming is a component of phonological awareness, which is the ability to identify and manipulate sounds in spoken words. Nursery rhymes are a common way to introduce young children to rhymes and help them develop phonological awareness skills. Identifying rhyming words does not require children to identify or manipulate sounds at the phoneme level, so it does not involve phonemic awareness. Additionally, it does not involve connecting the sounds to the letters that produce them, so it does not involve the alphabetic principle or phonics.

67. B: The floss rule states that the letters *f*, *l*, and *s* are doubled when they follow a short vowel sound. In choice B, the *s* is doubled because it follows an /ă/ sound. The remaining choices contain short vowel sounds but do not have a doubled *f*, *l*, or *s*.

68. B: Readers rely on prior knowledge and existing schemata to make sense of newly encountered texts. Therefore, texts that are more closely related to students' existing cultural schemata are more easily comprehended. To increase the likelihood of comprehension, the teacher should provide the student with background information on Thanksgiving before reading the book. Relating it to familiar traditions will also assist with activating the student's prior knowledge. Choice A does not provide any scaffolding to the student to assist with comprehension. Choice C offers some scaffolding in the form of a written outline, but it is less likely to be effective than an interactive discussion about the topic and the connection to the student's own cultural traditions. Choice D waits until after the book is read to offer additional information, even though it would be more beneficial to introduce the topic before reading.

69. C: Although teachers may supply the possible options, students are typically given choices about the books they read for literature circles. This helps maintain interest and engagement throughout the process. Students participate in literature circles in small groups, and there are usually multiple books being read and discussed throughout a classroom. Students are encouraged to lead the discussions and introduce questions and topics for analysis. Additionally, groups may change frequently as students finish books and move on to new texts.

70. D: Denotative meanings are the literal meanings of words found when they are looked up in the dictionary. Connotative meanings are the ideas or feelings evoked by the words. Therefore, two words can have the same denotative meaning in the dictionary, yet evoke very different reactions from readers. *Frugal* and *cheap* can both mean costing little, yet *cheap* often carries a negative connotation. For example, people may be insulted if they were called cheap, yet take pride in being referred to as frugal. The remaining pairs of words have similar meanings, and they all evoke positive feelings.

71. D: *Assonance* is the term used to describe repeated vowel sounds in nearby words. Assonance is often found in poetry and can be used to affect mood. Onomatopoeia refers to the use of sound words. Alliteration occurs when several words near one another in a text begin with the same sound. Consonance is a term used to describe repeated consonant sounds in nearby words.

72. D: Schwas are the unstressed, central vowel sounds commonly found in words, such as the sound produced by the *a* in *around*. Digraphs are two letters that form a sound. The term *digraph* refers to the groups of letters, not the sounds that are produced. When vowels make long sounds, they produce the sounds of their letter names. The *a* in *around* does not say its name. Diphthongs occur when two vowel sounds are combined within a syllable. The *a* in *around* does not have another vowel next to it that influences its sound.

73. C: The student has spelled all of the words correctly except for those with silent letters. Therefore, it would be most helpful to focus on silent-letter spelling patterns. Additionally, the student had no errors in subject/verb agreement.

74. C: When a word can be pronounced two different ways, reading the sentence twice and pronouncing the word each way can help the reader determine which pronunciation makes sense. For example, a student might encounter a sentence that says, "The mother put a bow in her daughter's hair." Knowing that *bow* can be pronounced two different ways, the student can read the sentence twice, pronouncing the word differently each time. That strategy should help the student identify which way makes sense. Choices A and B are incorrect because identifying known parts of the word using visual clues will not assist the reader with knowing which pronunciation is correct in the given context. Additional context clues from the surrounding text are needed. Choice D is incorrect because the student may know other *oo* words with both pronunciations, so again, additional context clues are needed.

75. D: A glossary contains an alphabetized list of important vocabulary words found in a text, along with their meanings. It is similar to a dictionary. It would be the most helpful text feature for a student to use to determine the meanings of the content-related vocabulary words in the text. The table of contents helps the reader identify which pages contain which topics in the text. Headings help the reader determine the main idea of each section of the text. The index is an alphabetized list of topics in the text, along with the page numbers on which they can be found.

76. A: *Story grammar* refers to the general structure of a story, including the beginning, middle, and end. It also includes basic story elements, such as character, setting, conflict, and resolution. Although it includes the word "grammar," story grammar focuses on the content of a story rather than its conventions or syntax. Additionally, while it may include some discussion of main idea, story grammar is much broader and includes many components of story structure.

77. B: Synonyms are words that mean the same thing. *Conceited* and *pompous* both mean overly proud of oneself. *Selfish* and *generous* are antonyms because they mean the opposite of one another. *Photograph* and *photosynthesis* both contain the same Greek root, *photo*, meaning light. The words *steel* and *steal* are homophones because they sound the same, but are spelled differently and have different meanings

78. D: Antonyms are words that mean the opposite of one another. *Drowsy* means to be sleepy, while *alert* means to be wide awake. Therefore, they are antonyms. *Build* and *construct* are synonyms because they mean the same thing. The two types of *peer* are homographs because they are spelled the same but have different meanings. *Shake* and *cake* are rhyming words.

79. B: Students are analyzing the structure of the word by identifying the prefix, root, and suffix. Miscue analysis refers to analyzing reading errors to determine patterns in the strategies that students are using. Syllabification refers to breaking words into syllables. Because the suffix *-ible* has two syllables, and students are focusing on the meanings of the word parts, they are not focused on syllabification. Decoding is the process of translating graphemes into phonemes, or letters into sounds. In this example, students are focusing on identifying the word parts and their meanings rather than on simply decoding and reading the word.

80. A: In the pre-alphabetic stage of word learning, children do not yet have an understanding of letter/sound relationships they can use to decode words. They may remember some words based on visual features, such as words found in environmental print. Choice B describes the partial alphabetic stage, when children begin to use letter/sound relationships to decode some sounds in words, particularly the beginning and ending sounds. Choice C describes the full alphabetic stage, and choice D describes the consolidated alphabetic stage.

81. D: Character maps, fact and opinion charts, 5Ws charts, and webs are all examples of graphic organizers, which are used to help students organize and visualize information, concepts, and relationships. Literary elements are components of fictional stories, such as characters and settings. Genres are categories of texts, such as biographies and fairy tales. Text features are parts of nonfiction texts, such as headings and graphics, that are used to organize the text and provide additional information.

82. B: Figurative language involves the use of words and phrases that differ from their literal meanings. The expression in choice B means that the wet snow covered the ground, not that it was literally a wet blanket. It is an example of a metaphor, which is one type of figurative language. The other options contain some descriptive words and phrases, but they have literal meanings.

83. D: Etymology is the study of word origins and history. Morphology is the study of word parts and word forms. Linguistics is the study of language and its structure. Semantics is a part of linguistics and involves the study of meaning in language.

84. B: Decodable texts use many words containing previously taught phonics skills, allowing readers to practice those skills in context while reading new books. They can be one component found in classrooms that use explicit phonics instruction. Choice A describes predictable books, which rely more on patterns in language rather than phonics skills, to assist readers with decoding. Because most words in decodable texts contain previously learned phonics skills, they do not often have content-related vocabulary words with more complex spelling patterns. Additionally, the focus is on using decodable words rather than on complex plot development, so they may not be appropriate for close reading activities.

85. C: CVC words, which contain a consonant, a short vowel, and another consonant, are typically taught before the other listed spelling patterns. These words are easy to decode for beginning readers. Long vowel sounds, such as those in choices A and B, are typically taught after short vowel sounds. Additionally, consonant blends and digraphs, as found in choice D, are also typically taught after CVC words.

86. C: Screening assessments are given to identify students who may be at future risk of academic difficulties and may benefit from interventions. Diagnostic assessments can then be given to confirm or provide additional information about screening results, including identifying students' specific strengths and needs. This information can then be used to guide instruction.

87. D: Analogies are used to help students recognize the relationships between words. Students are commonly given a pair of words whose relationship they must first identify. They then apply the same type of relationship to complete another word pair. Analogies can be used to help students recognize many different types of relationships, including recognizing synonyms, antonyms, and more. While students may explore word structure, definitions, and origins while completing analogies, the overall objective of analogies is to recognize and apply relationships between sets of words.

88. B: In this activity, students are identifying the discriminating phoneme in two words. In the example of *tap* and *top*, it is the middle phoneme that is different. To practice phoneme substitution, the teacher would give students a word and then instruct them to change one of the phonemes and identify the newly formed word. In phoneme deletion, the teacher would give students a word and instruct them to remove a phoneme and identify the newly formed word. In phoneme insertion, the teacher would give students a word and instruct them to add a phoneme and identify the newly formed word.

89. A: Progress monitoring is a type of assessment used to track students' progress towards certain goals over time. When students are receiving reading interventions, frequent progress monitoring should be done to assess their progress and determine if the interventions are succeeding. Screening is done initially to determine if students are at risk for academic difficulties, and it is done at greater intervals, such as the start of each school year. Summative assessment occurs at the end of a unit of study or other larger unit of instruction. Norm-referenced tests compare students' performances to the performances of sample groups of similar students, while progress monitoring is done to assess students' progress towards their own personal goals.

90. B: The pattern layer of orthography involves looking at groups of letters within words that form patterns. Therefore, exploring and building words that all contain *eigh* involves the pattern layer. The alphabet layer involves letter/sound relationships. The meaning layer involves the relationships between word meanings and their spellings. Conventional spelling refers to spelling words accurately.

91. C: Word walls should be flexible, meaning words can be removed if students have mastered them, and new words can be added as they are introduced. It is also helpful if the words on word walls are removable, so students can take them to other areas of the room when they are using them for reading and writing activities. Choice A is incorrect because there are many types of words that can be included on word walls, including content-related vocabulary, academic vocabulary, and high-frequency words. Choice B is incorrect because words can be displayed on word walls for different reasons. For example, words containing the same root can be displayed to help students see relationships between words. Because word walls can contain different types of words and be used for different purposes, they can be helpful for readers in all stages of reading development.

92. A: In the language experience approach, students decide on a story they want to tell and dictate it to a teacher, who writes the words down on paper. The teacher then reads the story back multiple times, modeling appropriate fluency. Students are then invited to join in reading the story. In writing workshop, students work on independent writing pieces following the stages of the writing process. They may all be involved in different stages at different times. Trait-based writing teaches students to consider the traits of good writing, such as word choice, throughout the writing process. During modeled writing, teachers think aloud as they record their thoughts on paper or on the board.

93. D: Reciprocal teaching is an activity in which students gradually take over the role of the teacher in small groups to discuss texts. The students lead discussions focused on four main reading strategies: summarizing, questioning, predicting, and clarifying. The remaining options are also reading strategies, but they are not typically the focus of reciprocal teaching activities.

94. C: Aesthetic response refers to a reader's personal interactions with a text. Rather than recalling information about the text, aesthetic response is personalized and based on the reader's own thoughts, feelings, and reactions. Choice C asks the readers to describe how a certain part of the story made them feel; therefore, it is focused on their aesthetic responses to the text. The other questions can be answered using information contained within the story rather than the readers' own personal reactions.

95. B: Anticipation guides are tools that are used to activate prior knowledge and help students build interest in a topic before reading. They typically consist of a series of statements about the topic, and students choose whether they agree or disagree with each statement. During reading, students note if newly learned information is changing their initial responses, and they reevaluate their initial responses after reading. A storyboard is a graphic organizer that shows individual scenes from a story in order. Concept maps are visual representations of the relationships between concepts, often displayed using a web-like format. An outline is a list of the main topics, subtopics, and details contained in the text.

96. C: A complex sentence has at least one dependent and one independent clause. A dependent clause cannot stand alone as a sentence, while an independent clause can. In choice C, the dependent clause is, "Before going to school"; while the independent clause is, "Michael brushed his teeth." Choice A is a simple sentence containing one independent clause. Choice B is a sentence with a compound predicate. Choice D is a compound sentence, meaning it contains two or more independent clauses joined by a coordinating conjunction or semicolon.

97. C: By using varied books for read-alouds and shared reading activities, the teacher can ensure that students are exposed to a variety of genres and text structures. During these activities, the teacher can also help students explore the features of these texts. Choice A can be used to support this instruction, but the posters alone are not as likely to be effective as actually exploring varied types of books. Choices B and D do not ensure that all students will actually explore different types of texts.

98. A: A compound word is formed when two or more words are joined together to create a new word with its own meaning. In choice A, *backyard* is a compound word because it consists of two smaller words, *back* and *yard*, joined together. None of the other options contain compound words.

99. D: In choice D, the root word, *argue*, drops its *e* before the suffix is added. The correct spelling of the new word is *argument*. In the other options, the root words remain unchanged when the suffix is added.

100. A: Choice A is Chomsky's theory of Universal Grammar, which essentially posits that all languages use a structure and that these structural rules are innate to humans. Put another way, humans are innately capable of and inclined to acquire the rules of language. Choice B refers to another theory, the Natural Order Hypothesis, which describes a predictable order in language acquisition, which is universal to language acquisition. Choices C and D do not describe any current theories of acquisition.

Constructed Response

1. Sample Response:

Caleb's response shows both some strengths and weaknesses with regards to his writing skills. He clearly has a strong understanding of sentence structure and alphabetic principle, and he knows how to spell many high-frequency words conventionally and apply several phonics skills. However, there are some phonics skills and spelling patterns that Caleb still needs to develop.

Caleb has divided his writing into complete sentences, and each sentence starts with a capital letter. He has also used periods, which are the correct ending punctuation, at the ends of all of the sentences. He has also used correct word spacing. All of these factors indicate that he has a strong understanding of concepts of print and basic sentence structure.

Caleb has also spelled many high-frequency words conventionally, including *my*, *we*, and *are*. Additionally, several of his misspelled words indicate the use of phonics strategies. Some of the misspelled words were spelled using other letters that make the same sounds. For example, he spelled *some* using the CVC spelling pattern *sum*, showing he is applying sound/symbol relationships to encode the word. This is also demonstrated in Caleb's spelling of the word *sour*, where he represented the middle sound using *ow* instead of *ou* because they often make the same sound.

There are a few areas where Caleb's writing shows weaknesses. He did not spell the *ed* inflectional endings correctly in the words *tasted*, *learned*, *walked*, and *looked*, so he would benefit from some practice in this area. He also omitted the last *e* in both *yesterday* and *cider*, indicating he could benefit from practice in r-controlled vowels, particularly *er*. Omitting the final *s* from *class* shows that he would benefit from learning the floss rule, which states that the letter *s* is doubled when it follows a short vowel sound.

2. Sample Response:

Alicia's responses to this assessment indicate both some strengths and weaknesses regarding concepts of print. She appears to have strong book-handling skills and awareness of book concepts, yet struggles with more difficult concepts, such as directionality and one-to-one correspondence.

Alicia showed strong book-handling skills by holding the book right side up. Additionally, she was able to correctly identify the front and back of the book, along with the title. These book-handling and book-awareness skills are typically some of the first concepts of print to be developed.

Alicia struggled with more complex concepts of print. When asked to identify the correct place to start reading, she turned to page three, when the text actually began on page one. In addition to not being able to identify where to begin reading the entire book, she incorrectly identified where to start reading on a single page by choosing a word in the middle of the sentence. The sentence on page three stated, "It is fun to run," and Alicia indicated that you should start reading beginning with the word *fun*.

By moving her hand back and forth rapidly in a zig-zag manner, Alicia indicated that she has not yet developed the concept of directionality, or the idea that print is read from left to right across the page. She also did not demonstrate an understanding of one-to-one correspondence, or the understanding that each printed word relates to one spoken word. This was evident when she was asked to point to the words while the teacher read, and she pointed to the same printed word three times while the teacher read three different words from the sentence aloud.